UNCERTAIN TOMORROWS

AUTOECOGRAPHY OF A STOLEN FUTURE - 1

UNCERTAIN TOMORROWS

FROM THE WATERS OF GODAVARI TO THE SANDS OF PILANI

Professor C B S R SHARMA

KALPAZ

ISBN: 978-93-5324-953-3 (HB)

First Published, 2022

Published by

Kalpaz Publications
C-30, Satyawati Nagar,
Delhi – 110052
Ph.: 011-47034999, 9811692060
www.kalpazpublications.com
E-mail: kalpaz@hotmail.com

Printed at: Gyan Press, Delhi.

DEDICATION

Mahidhara Venkata Satya Murty

My Mother's Younger Brother
Who laboured for years in Kesanakurru of Konaseema
to Initiate me into the Beauty of Education

Peddi

Domestic Help at Avidi village, Who
Financed my journey to Pilani
WITH HER LIFE'S SAVINGS OF Rs 460

Pranab Ray

A student Friend at Pilani
and The College Street of Calcutta
For the Spirit of Youth

ACKNOWLEDGMENTS

MAJOR INFLUENCES

1. Duvvuri Veerabhadram, School Teacher, Polavaram, Picked me from Standard 2 and guided me to win a seat in Standard 6
2. "Jagruti" Venkataramayya. School Teacher at Razole opened new worlds of literature and recitations of soulful poetry
3. Bhamidipati Parvateesam, Head Master at Manepalli, Cultivated in me to develop world views through Newspapers and share with others
4. Sardar Ajaib Singh Bhullar, An army officer deputed to the NCC of our college who motivated me to work hard and progress steadily.
5. Babu Narhar Muley, Professor of Botany, Pilani, Served as an Icon for values and a role-model in student care and humanism.
6. Lothar Wendel, Professor of German, at BITS, Pilani introduced me to the world of Literature and value-based politics of Europe.
7. M.S. Swaminathan and his team, IARI, New Delhi served as role models in conducting science and managing developments during my stay in his labs.

TIMELY HELP

1. Mamidisetty Chandranna and Suranna
   Our traditional peasantry
2. Penumarti Sree Rama Murty
3. Mahidhara Satya Murty
4. Saraswatula Suryanarayana
5. Vedavathi and Leela
6. Ajanta, Viswanatha Sharma
7. Lanka Ramasastry
8. Mamillapalli Suryanarayana
9. Peddi, our domestic help
10. C. Surendra Babu
11. Preetam Lal Sharma
12. B. D. Deshpande
13. B. V. Ratnam
14. B.N. Muley and Mummyji

THESIS TIME HELP

During my stay at Pilani during the Dussera vacation to submit my Ph.D thesis I was very well treated by all due to sympathy or goodwill or for a good riddance! I am indebted to all. Mr. S M M Rao and his wife were my hosts for excellent food and stay. My guide and warden Prof. Deshpande gave me space and furniture to keep my research luggages and work. Prof. S K Pillai corrected my manuscripts every day. Dr. Sankar Reddy, of Zoology department, later of Delhi University, painstakingly helped me with measurements of chromosomes to beat the deadline for thesis submission. Many students of Botany and Zoology helped me in many ways.

APOLOGIES AND THANKS

I must have forgotten many things I did go through. Only a fraction remains here. There will be those I did not partake. Hope others will fill these vast info in their works on Konaseema, before it is destroyed by the Railwayline and other anti-ecological developments.

Thanks are also to M M Sastry [Munganda], G N Rao [Krapa] and Meru Sarma [Kesanakurru] for their help with Script and Map and to Dr. Ramachandra Reddy [Ongole] for the References. The family tree, made by Shrimati Ramalakshmi was sent to me by her brother, Shri C.J. Shastri. This and the Jacket were designed by Mr. Dhanraj. Grateful to all of them.

REFERENCES

Maitland, Julia 1843. Letters from Madras, during the years 1836-39. O U P: 60-118.

Hemingway, F. R 1915. GODAVARI. Madras District Gazetteers, Government Press: 200-288.

LEGENDS OF PHOTOGRAPHS

PREFACE

This book is about my maturing through education, imparted at Schools, College and University. To this added is the childhood and the ecosystem freely interacting with people. The school begins; with all liking each other. While variations are first learnt, discriminations begin. But the great equalizers are the teachers rendering the journey enjoyable, for about a decade apparently interminable. This gift of providence ends, actors never to meet again!

Books on childhood were written by many. On journeys and travels many more appeared. But the present one is not a travelogue from the end of Godavari to which I belong, to the edge of Thar in Pilani where I completed my studies. But is a narrative of educational empowerment, concerned with society and its future. This is a story of hopes which ended in a glorious failure. After all the playfulness, the freedom of anarchy is taken away as if programmed.

Some of us, with the family culture, or yearning for elevations in life, or those with economic means, go to Colleges. This is a small percentage of the vast population of schooled children. Here adolescence begins. Endocrines function vigorously. Some have a college in their own towns. Some in nearby places. In other words, many schooled children have their families to cling even at the end of college. Many more do not have. These free birds acquire vagrancy and susceptible to vagabondage. Yet a few reach the niches, the Universities.

Yet all will experience reveries and dreams dispelling innocence and ignorance every day. The world appears full of best things ultimately summating into a good life. Guided education ends with hopes mixed with fears. This toss is the crux of life.

As the cruelty of the humans increase, comparisons become inescapable. Educational systems, man power, recipients all appear honest. But truth is otherwise camouflaging selfishness and cruelty ending in irreversible consequences. I had to search for comparability. The Piranahs were found to be more cruel than the spiders, snakes and the like.

Piranah is an Amazon fish known for a century to be one of the most dangerous of animals, thanks to Theodore Roosevelt, the then president of USA. He described a sight of Piranahs devouring a horse within 30 minutes in one of the tributaries of Amazon. Ever since similar reports appeared as well as some to the contrary. Variations in size, colour, diets as well as in virulence have been recorded ever since.

I did not suspect the sinning in education until I was doing research. Then I resolved that my education should be used to prevent misuses. Therefore the 1st part of the book becomes a preparation to face Piranahs. During employment I found unjust hostilities targeting me. Therefore the 2nd part develops as of conflicts. 3rd part deals with similar experiences, heard and read, and efforts to prevent the crimes and protect the victims. The 4th one is a re-evaluation of all, a kind of Psychoanalysis.

This is an autobiography. Most lives are made up by hereditary privileges, opportunities and self wills. Hindsight wisdoms tell us that most humans are products of circumstances, environment, niches, sub-consciences and economic handicaps. In other words, ecology becomes the determinant, heredity receding; converting an autobiography into an Auto-ecography.

The story of a life is an ecography or biography or both for different people. For most it is a welcome slavery, for its assured pleasures, absence of hard work and responsibilities. For me....it is the 3rd and 15th yogas of Bhagavatgita, taught by my mother during my childhood; A practise of ideal ecology.

why should we honour those
that die upon the field of battle,
a man may show as reckless a courage
in entering into the abyss of himself

– W. B. Yeats

CONTENTS

CHAPTER - 1

MY ECOSYSTEM

Godavari Delta, Konaseema
Cotton Seema or Seetamma Seema
Sunami or Uppena at Godavari Mouth
Rivers, Ferries, Beaches, Mangroves, Islands, Canals and Tanks

People and lives
Natives and Dalits
Migrants
Traditional Cultures and Christianity

Agriculture
Health Care
Education – Formal and Informal

Political Consciousness
Origin of Corruptions
Journalism
National Record in Murders
Communist Stories
Types of Communists

Behavioural Deviants
Historic Issues
Antarvedi Lands turned Fertile
Sukanya, the most gifted Devadasi

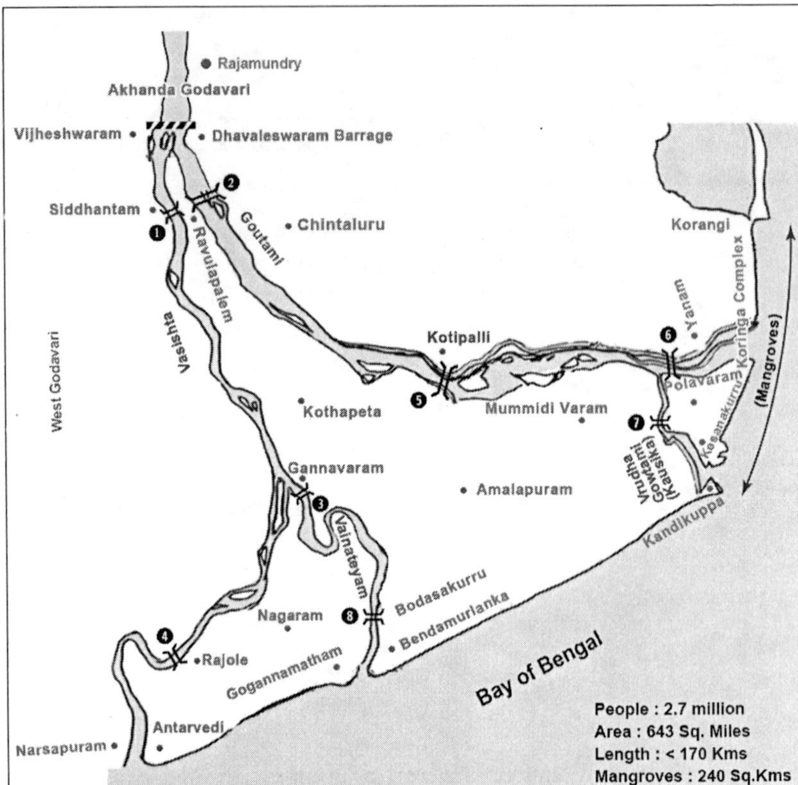

BRIDGES :

1 Siddhantam	3 Gannavaram	5 Kotipalli	7 Muramalla
2 Ravulapalem	4 Chinchinada	6 Yanam (Balayogi)	8 Bodasakurru

Fig. 2: Working Map of Godavari Delta commonly called KONASEEMA.

Fig. 3: Sir Arthur Cotton at Rajahmundry. This builder of the Dam on Godavari at Dhavaleswaram is the architect of the water distribution system with Canals, Tanks and regulators and became the mother of the Konaseema's Etherial Nature.

Fig. 4: Dokka Seetamma at Gannavaram Aqueduct is the Spirit and Ethos of Konaseema. Living in a Village Gannavaram at the junction of Vasishta and Vainatheyam, she was an Annadata, recognised by the British Queen.

There are so many beautiful things in the world. But the most enchanting one is the nature covering myriads of beautiful elements. One of them is water. Civilisations, most of them, began around water bodies; River valleys and deltas became cradles for the growth and development of human civilisations. These societies treated their cradles dear to heart, and dear to mind. One such is the Godavari Delta – popularly known as Konaseema, the corner region, into which I was borne and remained its child for ever.

GODAVARI RIVER AND TRIBUTARIES

Godavari that originates at Nasik in Maharashtra, branches into two after the town Rajamahendravaram in Andhra Pradesh - Gowthami and Vasishtha. Just before this point a Dam or Anicut was built connecting Dhavaleswaram in the north and Vrijheswarm in the south, by the British who also developed the delta. These two gradually become 7 tributaries before joining the Bay of Bengal forming 3 major Islands in the process. The three islands are : Polavaram, Amalapuram and Nagaram, separate from each other and with the mainland from times immemorial.

Vasishta flows ahead towards Antharvedi to join the sea. It gives a branch Vainatheyam at Gannavaram which flows until Bendamoorlanka where it joins the bay, Gowthami travelled further towards Yanam. It joined the sea as 5 branches – Kaasyapa [Tulyabhaga], Attri [Koringa], Viswamitra [Kousika], Jamadagni and Bharadwaja. after Nilapalli. The last three disappeared in time. At Vinjaram, before Yanam, Vrudhagowtami branches out until Kandikuppa, from where one travels by boats to reach the seashore. In the evening, returning will be on foot because there will be no water. This is due to ebbs and tides in water flow. These tide variations and salinity gave rise to Mangrove Forests.

Two aspects need to be noted here. Morning time waters are in high tide and boat has to traverse many islands – so small that they support only 2/3 huts, better called mounds. Secondly, no point was seen where the Vrudha Gowtami enters the sea as in Antarvedi and Bendamoorlanka. This raises a question whether this is a mere lateral intrusion of Gowtami or a tributary? Research efforts are warranted.

KONASEEMA

Konaseema is the delta of 3 islands between the tributaries of the Godavari River in the East Godavari District of Andhra Pradesh in southern India. It is nicknamed "God's Own Creation" due to its beauty. The Godavari delta is formed by - Vasishta, Vainateyam, Gautami, Vrudha Gautam and Koringa. The last is a highly divided feature full of Mangrove Forests. The three islands were gradually interconnected among themselves and with the mainland during the last 80 years by two aqueducts and 7 bridges. This was my world, my ecological niche for 19 years.

After crossing the city of Rajahmundry and the Dhavaleswaram Anicut, water is channeled to northern, southern and central regions. The last is considered

Konaseema and Bobbarlanka as its gateway. Amalapuram is the largest town, followed by Ravulapalem, Kothapeta, Razole and Mummidivaram.

COTTON SEEMA OR SEETAMMA SEEMA

Konaseema region from where the mangroves of Godavari begin from its northern island extending upto Kakinada port where the Upputeru joins the sea can also be called Seetamma Seema. Dokka Seetamma was well known for her character of freely serving food to the needy. She lived and served from the banks of Vainatheyam after it has just branched out from Vasista. This delta could have been christened as Cotton Seema more aptly, because of the chains of canals – Primary, Secondary and Tertiary, Tanks and other water bodies along with their associated vegetation, both crop and non-crop. This compounded charm generating a complex ethos of enduring fragrance would not have been possible but for the vision and services of Sir Arthur Cotton, a General of the Engineer Corps of England who built the Dhawaleswaram Anicut and all the associated structures.

Sir Arthur Cotton changed the whole scenario for better through development, as the leader of the project. The British decided to construct a barrage across Godavari between Dhavaleswaram and Vrijheswaram, raise the level of water and distribute to the lands needy for better agriculture. In a few years time canals left the Bobbarlanka region, the terminal point of the middle island, Amalapuram, and branched out. An aqueduct carrying water to southern island Nagaram was constructed at Gannavaram where Vasishta branched out as Vainatheyam. Another aqueduct was constructed at North of Annampalli where Gowthami branched into Vrudhagowthami to supply water to the Northern Island Polavaram. Thus, all the three islands were connected and water was distributed by Primary, Secondary and Tertiary canals, Regulators, Tanks etc. The entire land has only green cover with crops, vegetables, fruits, flowers, trees with water in all seasons, people who migrated earlier due to famines returned. Only floods and rains did not leave!

In gratitude and veneration, Sanskrit Scholars of this region composed a Slokam on Cotton and decreed to be recited while praying Sun God every morning in the river facing the Sun. There was none in history to whom veneration is expressed daily and periodically on every occasion. Sir Cotton turned Godavari, that carries every day 365 days of Thames, famine and flood prone into a delta of beauty and fertility of high magnitude in less than 5 years.

Dokka Seetamma lived near Gannavaram Aqueduct and was legendary for humanism by providing food to the needy at any time. She spent her resources, time and energy for fellow people. She was recognised, lauded and venerated. In fact, she is synonymous with the spirit of Konaseema, until the modern times arrived. The aqueduct at Gannavaram is named after her and her bust greets every one there just as Arthur Cotton on horse back does at Dhavaleswaram anicut.

SUNAMI OR UPPENA AT GODAVARI MOUTH

This area has seen many cyclones of different intensities, but also two oceanic upheavals - called UPPENA. The waters reached upto Samarlakota, this was the reason to lay the Howrah Railway line this far. Another uppena also occurred at Kalighattam [Calcutta]. It is at this time that some of the tributaries of Godavari-probably, Jamadagni and Bharadwaja, disappeared after Neelapalli. The same fate fell on the Godavari point - the meeting region of river and the sea.

WESTERN BANKS OF VASISHTA AND GOWTAMI

Undivided Godavari flew until the end of Rajahmundry, where the Anicut was built. Interestingly, the river bifurcates into two after the dam - Dhavaleswaram on the North and Vijjeswaram in the south. The northern one is called Gowtami and runs until Yanam after which it divides too much and runs into sea. Villages between these two towns on the western banks of Gowtami are similar in most respects with the land and people on the opposite side that makes the Konaseema. Most people therefore associate these western villages with Konaseema. And no one objects! The southern river is called Vasishta, and continues until Narsapuram before joining the Bay of Bengal. The land and people in the habitations along the western side of Vasishta are more similar to and active with Konaseema proper and therefore treated as Konaseema. For example, Celebrities Bapu of Narsapuram and Ramana of Dhawaleswaram are considered a Konaseema Duo! Inter-bank ferry services are one of the most fascinating aspects of water transport in these parts.

EARLIEST LIFT IRRIGATION BEYOND BOBBARLANKA

In recent times, lift irrigation is resorted to carry water spending a lot of valuable energy. But it should not be done without careful thinking and analysis of data, purposes and history. As back as 1960s I saw a small Lift irrigation system, south of the Dam at Bobbarlanka, less than 10 miles and looked unusual. The officials told that it is a valuable land getting copious rains, but the land should not be wasted for tank purposes. Therefore is water lifting was resorted to for agriculture and drinking.

CANAL SYSTEM FOR DRAINAGE

Many places on earth do not have water, or do not get by any means. This delta was not getting water enough although so much around. But subsequently a dam came, water level raised, canals were dug and water became surplus in the crop fields. What to do with the excesses for they could be harmful. Then came drainage as a study, canals for it as a new means. Drainage canals were even used for transport of materials if not humans. A whole philosophy of life was covert here.

BIRDS AND NESTS

In villages many houses maintain Rice grains for sparrows, and allow them build nests. Now almost disappearing, because both the birds and their consciousness in people are vaning. Bird nests in the wild hanging to the – Acacia, Toddy palms, etc can be seen. Sights at Nagaram are a phenomena by themselves.

RIVERS, FERRIES, BEACHES, MANGROVES, ISLANDS, CANALS AND TANKS

The three islands of Polavaram, Amalapuram and Nagaram with Godavari tributaries, and canal and tank systems built by Cotton, good rainfall, flora and fauna and people everywhere make this piece of geography very beautiful and inspires the innermost emotions of people. Along the nearly 180 km stretch of the land, there are many beaches good for human interactions – Antarvedi, Mori, Bendamoorlanka, Kandikuppa etc. One of the best points of meeting between river and sea is at Antarvedi, the southern tip of Konaseema. This can also be seen at Vodalarevu and Kandikuppa.

Mounds of average hight are formed near Kandikuppa. These support 2-3 huts on each. In high tide people use boats and freely walk during low tides, a very rare aspect of nature. After these, mangroves stretch towards Yanam and Kakinada through Koringa, another tributary of Gautami after Nilapalli off Yanam.

A Heaven on earth: Razole river ferry with cement steps, a Bodhi or Ravi Tree on the banks [*Ficus religiosa*] with a cement Platform. An ascetic sits there, with some followers, mostly singing philosophical Poetry of saints, called "Tatvams". After a few feet along the river flow, on the banks was a Park – a Radio, a natural lawn, some flowering plants, Jasmine, Night queen; breeze one gets only on Yamuna, waters and boatmen around. Occasionally, a steam launch sirens the coming times.

One of the finest moments in the lives of people could be the time one spends in Razole during evenings in front of a cinema hall, Ravi Picture Palace. This hall is on the canal bank the canal with boat and steamer service. On the other side of the canal is the embankment meant to prevent the flooding waters. There were about a score of Casuarina trees and the floor is full of grass forming a natural lawn. A good breeze and a music characteristic of the tall Casuarinas. This environment always invites visitors to spend 1-2 hours every day. Why?

The cinema hall plays music, normally unavailable in most places, before the evening show. This music is enjoyed by many people, including me, sitting on the natural lawn, hearing the sounds of passing waters and the serenades of the Casuarina grove. What is that Music? Private songs of Saluri Rajeswar Rao such as Challagalilo and of Ghantasala such as Pushpavilapam, Kuntikumari, poems of Satya Harishchandra, etc.

Who can remain unmoved by this fantastic combination of moving waters, serenading breeze, a lawn under a grove of Casuarinas and this soulful music ? That little piece of river front is just ethereal lulling people into imaginary worlds.

Why am I writing about a god-forsaken little place of no importance? Many might wonder in the same way! This is a yearning of heart. There will be no reasons. Only feelings, in the Cinema GLADIATOR, the mind of the Victim- Hero often goes to his native land serene, natural, with vegetation and wife and child, signifying nothing to the movie-goer but only to the hero! In the same vein I feel the loss of this paradise of nature, people, and life to - hypocrisy, cruelty, dishonesty, injustice, sadism, lying, in all walks of life including in the last bastion – Universities, unfortunately. For all miserable lives, Konaseema we lived was a heaven!

Konaseema is not only a combine of 3 bigger islands – but also of many smaller islands of considerable variety, probably 50 to count. Some have 2-3 Villages. Most have just a single village. Further most of these are surrounded by Godavari. And a few have sea on one side and Godavari on the other sides. Most of these support Cocoanut, Banana or Casuarina and Cashew nut. Many having saline water on one side support Mangroves. Some are uninhabited although agriculture and tree cultures are maintained. Pichikallanka is an example nearest to Dhavaleswaram Dam. Another typical example could be the Pallam island saturated with people [front cover]. Beaches are motorable and therefore special.

Boat races at Balusutippa, Cock Fights in the groves of Coconuts and Mangoes on the banks of Godavari, Bullock Cart Races in the rice fields after harvests and playing cards – all occasional and / or Seasonal - all with bets – are some of the pastimes.

Mud Crabs, eels or snake fish and Polasa Fish are very common. At Antarvedi, the region of maximum variety of catches from sea are auctioned and transported to other districts.

G. N. Rao hailing from Krapa in Guntur district, brought up in Konaseema, studied in Warangal, mostly worked in Madhya Pradesh, the best state of India in culture, responds to my script. It is this man whose mother happily donated for a common cause of farmers about 50 Sovereigns of gold about 70 years ago. He describes the boat ride from Gannavaram

> *"Watch the ups and downs of the song, how it goes like a boat in the Godavari. The commercial boat moves thus from Rajahmundry to Gannavaram. It is pulled by a couple of people adept in this art using the ropes made in Tottaramudi near Mukteswaram . In between you get the famous curd from the Lolla Laku [Locks], in the midst of the sounds of water filling in between the two gates of the Lock, and then Pullamma garu purchasing a half anna curd in a muntha [Earthen Potlet] and feeding us with the Dibba rotti, Oh, I just want to go back to those days, when irrespective of castes, they used to respect and love each other and you may not believe that Pullammagaru is well known and famous in that route Gannavaram to Rajahmundry and back, She never took us on the Rahdari Padava [Passenger Boat] as it was a bit costly and took us always by the Samanla Padava [Goods boat containing products of Coconuts and Banana and tins of Nuvvula Nuni [Sesame oil] from Komalavari*

Ganuga [extracting machine] of Munganda Agrahaaram. You feel so great to be a part of those wonderful days, and the love, respect and that feeling of affection towards each other breaking the caste barriers...."

"you say, I don't speak or express myself and only listen to others, but the fact of the matter is, every person in this world had feelings, sufferings, insults, only thing, some express and some take it silently, and the life goes on, but people do remember you for the good or bad things you committed, even after you left this world."

PEOPLE AND LIVES

These three islands are now connected with each other by bridges adjacent to the existing aqueducts or nearby. The water transport is reduced and human movements increased. Further the islands are connected to the mainland to go to Kakinada, Rajahmundry and Vijayawada. The geographical beauty is compromised! In this process the water transport for cultivation as well as human and animal consumption is also reduced rendering canals remnants of past beauties and utilities.

Yet some spots endearing to human heart still exist – the water in all its states, the seasons with their specific characteristics, coastal vegetations, crops and their associated cultures, festivals and festivities leaving a lot for individual curiosities to probe and enlighten themselves.

NATIVES AND DALITS

Being islands and many forested by mangroves, human habitations have been less historically. Nature must have allowed only fisher-folk, boatmen and sea-farers. Land should have some endemic flora and fauna. These lands must have been home to medicinal plants and cotton, varieties of cocoanut, Banana, sugarcane, rice, reeds and water plants. People who found the plants and animals useful only should have been living for long. In other words nature dependent working classes only must be inhabiting these habitats. The arrival of the French and the British provided catalysts for further populating these habitats. Obviously the elite communities must have come much later, for, they need other communities to be dependent upon, who depend on nature, on the other hand.

I had many class mates. They are of different varieties and backgrounds. Krishna Sastri and John Bullayya at I. Polavaram and George Suvarna Raju at Rajole, Narayana Swamy and John at Amalapuram were different from others and similar to each other. They are polite and courteous. Always talk of Ambedkar. They ask questions that are embarrassing. So I got interested in this group of people called Harijans by Gandhi but call themselves, Dalits. After years of observation and study I concluded that, among the Dalits of India, those from Konaseema must be the best, in many respects.

The earliest known to me was the Supernatural Balayogi of Mummidivaram, just a Yogi in Samadhi who does not communicate. He became legendary. Then came the Bojja family. Appalasamy of Kandikuppa was affluent due to the earnings of his *father from Burma who constructed a palace at Kandikuppa.* This is also the place of Akasam Family, the Zamindars of that area with a status fitting palace. Because he liked the person and poetry of Devulapalli Krishna Sastry, he named his first son Krishna Sastry who incidentally was a year senior to me in the school at I. Polavaram. I remember him organising student protest in 1953 when – Potti Sree Ramulu died fasting for a separate Andhra State from Madras Presidency. His close friend then was John Bullayya, my class mate. I visited his Malapalli with my uncle several times organising hygiene and sanitation programmes. He later migrated to Yanam to become a Manager of a Liquor shop and fostering a girl from Kshatriya community. Appalasamy named his second son as Tarakam after an exemplary Education Officer. Tarakam became gradually a focal point for societal protests and dissenting voices. Appalasamy became a member of Assembly several times and contributed his might for many social causes.

Another was Bayya Suryanarayana Murty [B.S. Murty] who became a Minister in Nehru Cabinet. He is from Mamidikuduru. From this very same place was Boyi Bhimanna, the poet who longed and sang for liberation of man! Others who hailed from this Nagaram island were Ganji Nageswara Rao and Kaneti Mohana Rao, the communist leaders and legislators. The latter was a friend of my uncle in Munganda, very talented.

Significantly he was a member of the first Parliament. They speak very chaste Telugu and keep neighbourhood always clean – both rare in most places.

MIGRANTS

Migrants from other regions of India constitute an interesting feature. Their contributions to the regional life are a subject of interest. Being a delta area, this region attracted the attention of all rulers due to its water and fertility – Arcot Muslims, British and the Brown sahibs abandoned by the former kings and chieftains. The deterrent is the excess of water in the form of regular rains and floods and occasional marine tides of high intensity. Obviously famines too induced re-migrations.

The migrants are Brahmins, Kshatriyas, Vaishyas, Chieftain and Agricultural communities from far and near.

BRAHMINS

They came from all sides – Niyogis, Vaidikas and the Dravidas, primarily. The Dravidas came from Kaveri region through land and waterbodies and settled in Nellore, Amalapuram and Anakapalle. From the latter some migrated to Vijayanagaram. They are called Pudur, Dimili, Arama, and Perur dravids. Some from Kumbhakonam went to Palghat. They are maintaining their advaita individuality allegiance to Sri Sankara even now. Peruru near Amalapuram, Ryali beyond Kothapeta represent them. They further migrated towards

Visakhapatnam and spread to other villages in these three islands.

Another migrant from the south are the Vaishnavas, the Vishishtadvaitis. They were scattered in many places along the coastline like the others but in smaller number with definite character and purpose. They became mostly the priests of temples built for Vishnu. Their allegiance has been to Sri Ramanuja and practised Traditions – living, language, learning. education. healthcare, music, natya and the like. Of course these expertises gradually spread. These Ayyangars who limited themselves to Vaishnava temples are more pious, specialising in health, medicine and music. Sometimes they conducted schools for children. They are venerated and taken care by society.

The Niyogis and Vaidikas came along the river Godavari, obviously from Marathi and Hindi regions. Some were in the employment of the local Chiefs – from landlords to kings. Others lived and functioned under the patronage of the same local lords, ostensibly. These together migrated until Rajamahendravaram / Kovur and distributed to different regions, the Nadus. Thus, came the Natlus – Vegi, Vela, Kosala, Mulaka, Telaga, etc; similarly, the Niyogis, too. Niyogis had a history of serving the rulers which became a tradition in time. Correspondingly their practices of Brahmin rituals decreased because they have to give their time to the administrative responsibilities. Otherwise they too are vaidics following advaita dharma. The Dravidas and the Vaishnavites are also Vaidikas – practicing the vedic dharma and chores. Originally settled in a few places –

the agrahaarams. Subsequently, shifted to other places in small groups.

The agrahaarams used have mostly Brahmins. They are very few currently. Konaseema has three such Gangalakurru, Munganda and Perur. The Jamindar of Perur stated in 1953, while establishing the now famous SKBR College that "our forefathers came from Kaveri area. We were always treated by you as one of you. We pay our indebtedness to this region by establishing this college that may be useful to people of this Konaseema".

They greatly modified the language – both vocabulary and speaking style. Some musical intonation crept in. they became leaders of learning, language, music. natya, education, healthcare, and what not. The way the language is spoken in this region, even today is very special. All castes and religions still represent this classical brand of Telugu.

Konaseema used to be famous for 3 agraharams of Brahmins. Munganda agrahaaram consists of Veginati Brahmins, known for stupidity, craziness and cynicism. Gangalakurru is full of Velanadu sect of Brahmins, saner and focused, therefore accomplished. The third is Peruru Agrahaaram consisting of Dravida sect of Brahmins; most conservative and disciplined. All three have Tanks and an organised community.

Telugu was spoken here even from those days in a sing-song manner. This regional variant is either made fun-of in the rest of Telugu land or venerated. Chief character here is Sarcasm – biting at that – not known elsewhere.

Another distinguished feature is the culinary diversity, perhaps unknown anywhere in Andhra, or India and perhaps in the world. With the variety of plants the recipes go; with the richness in nature the leisure is promoted and with leisure the art of gastronomy, besides laziness.

One cannot generalise any one on any issue; more so as a whole. Brahmins of several types, origins, vocations, professions, predominantly are associated with scholarship and education. They were generally inappropriate with us. My grand father was not allowed to complete his studies by his mother and sister! He was simple and innocent that people exploited fully and impoverished him. At the end of it they derided him, poked fun, looted his academic properties. At the end of it all he spent his Provident Fund to buy books for children. Every one used them, did not return; yet condemned his foolishness in buying books, that too in an Agrahaaram. The same fate fell on me, people pilfered my books, helped by my brothers and mother! I rarely found one who rejoiced at my progress in education including relatives. However good, it is the financial status that determines the kinships. Of course exceptions have been experienced.

VAISHYAS

These are of two types. The telugu- speaking traditional Komatis from other non-island people who came to expand their professions. The other migrants include the traditional money-lenders in India, the

Marwari Vaishyas. While the former is within the language group the latter is pan-Indian. This was also a reason for the growth of Indian-ness in an otherwise very diverse peninsula. It is because of this merchant class, it is believed that Ambajipeta, south of Amalapuram, an important trade-post has come up and named after Amba.

KSHATRIYAS AND VALOUR OF WOMEN

To me, Kshatriyas are the noblest, frankest and kindest. Education was picking up which was not a fancy with them earlier. Datla brothers in Kesanakurru, Varma Brothers at Muramalla, and some families in Chintalapalli near Razole are some examples. I found excellent people in Polavaram, Thanelanka, Allavaram, Atreyapuram, Malkipuram, Antarvedi, etc. Noble and kind and do not talk much. Buchikrishnam Raju of Polavaram has maintained a huge library in the first floor of his Palace. It is here I perused through the great book, Andhra Sarwaswamu. Probably this is the biggest library in Konaseema at that time. Most of them stand for values, which currently have begun to fade.

I always considered, like many before me that the western banks of Vasista as well as of Gowtami are parts of Konaseema heritage and culture. An example is here. During early 1950s Konaseema was beset with several political and social issues. One was the declared termination of Zamindari system resulting in higher expectations from the traditional tenants and resistances from the land-owners. One such area was Malkipuram, especially the Kshatriya community. The owners are leadered by Rudraraju Ramalinga Raju, a Congress man. The down-trodden was supported by Alluri Venkatarama Raju. Further the political sufferers were given lands by the government, but are being usurped by the local leaders and given in stead, some useless ones. The sufferers here also were supported by Venkataramaraju. Many of his relatives and supporters live across the river, in Yelamanchili, Ootada, Chinchinada, Narsapuram, Palakollu, etc. – all in the West Godavari district.

Justice is with this vast majority. But the power is with RRR! As he is a Congress man. He called all others communists and controlled them through police. Those were the days of Telangana Liberation and communists were ruthlessly suppressed. The police arrested, tortured and killed under the guidance of RRR. Most of the victims were his own relatives, known people and of his community. His opposition was eliminated. Many Kshatriya families around Narsapuram and Palakollu lost their earning members, young women became widows, but they were never won by RRR. The communist leadership of the state came to Narsapuram to take stock of the situation.

Kshatriya women who used to practice "Ghosha" system, i.e. not to be seen outside their houses, came in large numbers to Narsapur. Dozens of boats travelled across Vasista from the eastern side – Razole, Malkipuram, Ramaraju Lanka, Antarvedi, and Sakhinetipalli carrying the victims and their supporters to Narsapuram. All these marched the streets of Narsapuram formed the audience of the meeting addressed by Sundarayya, Mukdom, and others. Such a procession by women under veil has happened only once after in Ratnagiri in Maharashtra, but by Muslim women. The Banyan tree, to which many Rajus were tied and shot during these times became a sacred area for visitations. And I too did ! Both the banks of Godavari are just one.

The author is very happy to recollect his family's association with Kaakarlapudi Zamindari of Ramachandrapuram as well as of Island Polavaram. Buchikrishnamraju's brother has come to Ramachandrapuram on adoption and improved the Draksharama temple of which he was the trustee. Another family was that of Datlas of Pattipadu, Tuni and Kesanakurru and Mudunuri of Muramalla.

NAIDUS

Kapus, called naidus also are the largest single community among the Telugu speaking people. Historically they are the leaders of platoons of Kings, small and big. Among the additional duties was the protection and guarding properties of sorts, the Kapala. They were the famous rulers of Madurai region for many decades. Once the kingdoms vanished they are reduced to the levels lords of land obtained from the past masters. Thus, emerged a community of great variation and class of people. They are agriculturists along with secondary professions, what-not! Generally conscious of self help and helping fellows in the community, their pride keep them shine individually and prevent them from unity.

This is why political power eluded them despite their numbers and regional and local popularities.

I have a very large number of friends in Polavaram, Kesanakurru, Manepalli, Amalapuram, Kothapeta, Bobbarlanka, Mandapeta etc. They often excel in arts and drama and keep Devadasis as collaterals. Many of their conflicts often due to this factor in rural societies.

The last category of migrants is the workers of all sorts including fields; all others come under this category – even those who work as soldiers and their leaders working under vassal kings, local chiefs, etc. Agriculturists and other professionals belong to this category. These field workers who go wherever there is work.

Thus, Konaseema has the native population of workers closely connected with the nature while immigrants mostly were the so-called upper castes and classes who depend on the former.

THE CULTURES

There are all the three major religions of India – Hindu, Muslim and Christian along with sects and sub-sects - all freely practicing their faiths. Temples of Siva, Vishnu and village Deities, Churches and Mosques are scattered widely.

Also secular Yogis, Ascetics with philosophies of common sense also present – several followers of Potuluri Veerabrahmendra Swamy in Razole, Kottalanka Yogi, a muslim ascetic and Mummidivaram's Balayogi, a harijan in Gandhian nomenclature. Organisations adherent to

Sringeri Sankaracharya, Shirdi Saibaba, Satya Saibaba, coexist in this small area!

The cultures and festivals also had the variations reflected in their performance – every one enjoying every one else's variants! Festivals such as Sankranti, Sivaratri, Ramanavami, Krishnashtami, Vinayakachaviti, Vyasa Poornima, Sanitrayodasi, Radhasaptami, Dussera, Deepavali, etcetera are celebrated joyfully through, Harikatha, Burrakatha, Tolubommalata, Buttabommalata, Kolatam, Bhogam Melalu, Teerthams, Karrasamu, Kattisamu, Kodipandelu, Eddupandelu, Boat-races and what not. With time many are modified and some vanished. Prabhala Teerthalu are a glory of Sankranti.

Dance and Music practitioners functioning as teachers, Geddam family of Vakatippa, for long trained Devadasis. Many brahmins practiced and taught music. But the greatest musician Mangalampalli Balamuralikrishna shifted to Vijayawada leaving Kadali and Sankaraguptam. Avasarala Satyavati and Eemani Sankara Sastry and Mahendravada in Music, Vedic Scholars – Uppuluri, Merusomayajula, Khandavalli, Nadiminti, Pulya, Mahidhara, Sripada etc. Mahidhara Gopala Krishnayya, Ajanta Penumarti Viswanatha Sharma, Mahidhara Ram Mohan Rao, Vemparala Suryanarayana Sastry, Madhunapantula and Chellapilla in literature and Nishtala Brothers in Burrakatha, were some of the illustrious names Priya Sisters and Geeta Madhuri appear to be from this land.

Devadasi Annabattula Satyabhama of Mummidivaram had visitors all through her life to learn Bhama-

and Gollakalapam. Every year Connoissers of culture used to meet in Bucchamma Agraharam, where Chellapalli Venkata Sastry would gift the dancer Rs 116 – an honorable deed in those times with a comment "Every where I receive gifts such as these, but this is the only place where you take from me!" Harikatha maestro the beautiful Devadasi of Manepalli nurtured by Jayanti Pantulu Garu of Pedapatnam is another example.

Kompella Janardana Rao, Gutala Krishna Murty, Adurti Subba Rao. Turaga, Garimella, Vadrevu, Alluri, Rudraraju, Nalla families, three Sattirajus – Pogaku, Sirangi, and Akkala. Bojja, Akella, Bolla and Bikkina are some significant families. The Muslims of Nagaram is a class by itself not only for Konaseema but for the whole Telugu Nadu.

TRADITIONAL CULTURES AND CHRISTIANITY

This region is full of Folk Gods, Puranic Gods, Temples, Chariots, Teerthams, Prabhas, Garagas, Asadis, Priests, Worships, Sacrifices, Propitiations. Many Temples mostly of Folk Gods, Churches of different persuasions and economic strengths. Christianity began in the delta area, probably with the arrival of the British to these parts. Conversions were taking place by the time of independence and stabilised very soon. Currently this is one of the busiest places in converting lower most castes into Christianity despite Ambedkar ethos.

TEMPLE CHARIOTS AND TRADITIONAL RIGHTS

Konaseema is full of temples – small and big and in between. Every village has at least one. Most of these have their special festive occasions in addition to the common ones. Some of these have chariots on which the deity goes about visiting his domain. And there are specific traditions about this factor.

The Marakallu have special privileges on temple chariots. They only pull with the ropes they make from cocoanut fiber. They also make fibre from cotton too. They make the Chariot with the wood they select. They only repair. They also make boats. They rarely go to sea or fish although they are not forbidden. They are considered and venerated as the children of water God, Ganga, the mother of Bhishma, the hero of Mahabharata, the fifth Veda.

Recently there was an incident of chariot burning at Antarvedi big temple. The culprits were never caught. From the historical facts, it is my belief that some Marakallu did it with the support or encouragement from the authorities. But these Marakas must be interested in its repairs or new construction and wages. And these people may not be devotees of the deity any more. Therefore, my hunch is that some people historically connected with temple traditions pertaining to Chariots only have indulged in this vandalism only for economic gains through political supports. And they no longer must be believers in their traditional god.

FROM TRADITION TO REFORMS

My name is a long one. Why so. I am to be named after my grand father, Seeta Ramayya. On the day of Namakaranam, My maternal grand father found that "Sun" is week in my horoscope; so Bhaskar has to be added. "Moon" was also weak. "Chandra" , too came in. All these added up to "Bhaskara Sita Ramachandra" preceded by a surname and followed by a caste indicating tail, Ultimately a formidable combine. This is the norm everywhere in our area in those times.

Andhras were historically fond of Bengalees, especially the upper castes. One family is full of "Sagars" after Iswar Chandra Vidya Sagar and another with " Mohans" after Ram Mohan Roy. Many families named their daughters beginning with Su.... after the Tagore's many women characters in his literary works. – Subhashini, Suhasini, and so on. Gandhi, Bose, Lenin and Stalin are also very popular. Bojja Appalaswamy, our MLA, named his first son "Krishna Sastry" after a great Telugu Poet, Devulapalli Krishna Sastry.

Reforms touched marriages too. A brahmin girl from Munganda married a Kamma man from Achanta with the blessings of a few brahmins. Another Brahmin man from the same village married a Kamma girl from Chinchinada, whose marriage was solemnised by the great Communist Sundarayya at Narsapuram, in public. This couple later started a Kammavari Agrahaaram near Srikakulam ! Another Brahmin girl married a Kshatriya man.

AGRICULTURE

The region is famous for its vegetation, most of them useful and therefore connected with people. Many plants specially cultured elsewhere can be seen here growing wild and consequently used freely – Guava, Citruses, Sapota, Custard Apple, Pomegranate, even Mangoes until recently. Both Toddy and Cocoanut in all its forms are available. Most people are not aware of the Cocoanut Variety "Gangabondam" comes from the terminus of Vainatheyam, whose genes spread world wide in many short varieties.

This can be spoken of as *in situ* agriculture – something useful grows wildly everywhere for leaves, fruits, nuts, roots, rhizomes. Almost every village will have an expert in medicinal plants and practice. In short this region is a source of Germplasm for many of today's cultivated plants. There are about 20 types of Bananas alone. The sea-front is home for mangroves which are disappearing with governmental support !

Bullock carts and boats pulled in the canals used to carry paddy, cocoanuts, bananas, mangos, and their products and other vegetable products – pulses and oil seeds, etc. We used to travel on these free to Rajahmundry and destinations before.

Weekly markets are a phenomenon probably not new only for Konaseema, for they are heard from several parts of India. But the uniqueness of this tiny place is that weekly markets are held on all the 7 days – in different places on each day. Sankaracharya of Sringeri when he toured Konaseema in a Golden Palanquin, commented that this must be god's own place because there is a cheap, socialistic market on every day helping people spend much less money than anywhere else in places he has seen ! These markets are limited only to some suitable villages. In most of these, touring talkies were there to entertain people with Cinema. It must be mentioned specifically that this tiny place is a great attraction for Cinema Shootings.

The Co-operative Bank [SKCC] initiated as a part of the Co-Operative movement of the Congress, was run by that partys leaders, normally rich peasantry. Soon this became another power centre in every village, that helped the farmers easy credit at low interests. Sri Kala Venkata Rao used to be a Minister in the capital; when not, the president of this bank.

HEALTH CARE and SERVICES

Ayurveda, Homeopathy, Unani and Scientific medicines were practiced in that order of priority. As times passed, tradition gave way to modernity and continues. There is only one major hospital at Amalapuram. But almost all villages will have one Ayurvedic doctor - would even make the drugs. The priests of temples are often good in health matters too. The Vaishnava priest with 111 on his forehead, invariably used to give drugs. In due course, the British introduced Certificate and Licentiate courses, short term. Ayurveda being a heritage or tradition, these courses revolutionised ill-health recoveries. However, the tantric and occult practices continued simultaneously, until the Tantric Doctor fell ill. These are practised both by Hindus as well as Muslims ! Trained Doctors are very few – Mantha Subba Rao in Amalapuram, Amanchi Rama Rao and K T Raja Rao in Rajole and Khandavilli Dikshitulu in Munganda. They only held a MBBS degree for a longtime. Others were – LMPs and RMPs in 3-4 places more, the most distinguished being Ambarkhana Sree Rama Murty at Kothapeta, about whom one can write a "Motorcycle Dairies" like Gevera, because of his fondness of Motor Cycle to visit patients.

There were many people, teachers, religious priests, temple priests, who knew about human body, and plants of utility to man etc, who practiced caring for human health. This aspect was noticed by the British to develop LMP and RMP courses by adding some from their practices. Yet, there are not enough of doctors in this region, for many reasons. There were only 6 doctors with a MBBS degree and a few more with other diplomas. There were some practitioners of Unani system and Homeopathy. One village has 3 doctors and that too on the same road which is therefore christened as Red Cross Street.

There are two significant features of medicine this region has been proud of and carried to posterity. First is the Chintaluru tradition by the Dwibhashyam Family from the head region of Gowtami, but from the western bank, which is also considered as Konaseema due to the continuity from the eastern bank through waters. This tradition continues for generations as a heritage. Second is the Vijjeswaram tradition from the head region of Vasista, again from the Western Bank. This is by the Achanta Family and its head, Ayurveda Bhishagwara Achanta Lakshmipathi was a nationally famous doyen of Ayurveda. He was reputed to have performed Surgery like Susruta, at Madras.

He shifted to this city and trained hundreds of doctors to serve the people. His wife was also a trained doctor who became a health minister in Madras Presidency. In recognition of their contributions two streets were named after them. Interestingly while Lakshmipathi was famous for scholarship, experimentation, innovations and the like, the Chintaluru clan concentrated on drugs and their manufacture and distribution, which continues even today.

The most illustrious doctor especially for women was Dr. Goteti Saraswati. Gradually her whole family entered the medical profession. There was no family dedicated to people's health as hers. And she was only a diploma holder from Kolkata. Her family probably hailed from the village Avidi near Kothapeta.

The doctor on the move is from Kothapeta. He is well known as the traveling doctor, for his almost daily journeys on his Bullet to see his patients all around his home town for around 10-15 km each side. A tall dark athletic handsome man was assisted by his brother. Later he was joined by his son, a sub-junior to me in the college at Amalapuram. He was our doctor, although both my brother and father died despite his treatment. But he was an ideal and dedicated RMP doctor, the kind of which are rare. He only told me that "your father was recovering. But the attacks by the Jaggannapeta people worsened his condition, utterances against you hurt him too deeply and we lost him".

7000 - DOCTORS

An interesting epithet. Do not mistake this for a production or descent of so many doctors all of a sudden. But all of a sudden many youngsters joined for medicice, if their parents had the ability to pay Rs 7000 as a donation to the newly starting Rangaraya Medical College at Kakinada. Many of my class mates, many weaker than me, joined here. For some time they were made fun off, only to be accepted as a reality and then a necessity.

During the early '60s, a well equipped hospital was established by the Christian missionaries with American aid mostly for the use of Women and Children. This institution has revolutionised the outlooks of people at large vis-à-vis health of people.

EDUCATION - Formal and Informal

The best in these islands is the education. Beginning with Sanskrit, graduating with Veedhibadis [Street Schools], Temple Schooling, some landlords opened elementary schools, upgraded them to middle schools, and thence to high schools, by generous donations, of course for avoiding land reforms and obtain good name among people keeping the future elections in mind ! Who ever knows something is willing to teach. In 1950, quite soon after independence, a regionally popular Congress leader's son Ramabhadra Raju from Allavaram, and one of the Zamindars appropriate to the locality, Bhanoji Ramars of Peruru, belonging to the migrant Ayyar clan of Kumbhakonam, build this famous college of mine SKBR College, at Amalapuram 70 years ago.

POLITICAL CONSCIOUSNESS

Despite the riverine obstructions winds of thought and change moved into these islands. Some went to Taluka or district capitals to join the freedom movement. Some went to state capitals. Some continued within islands. These depend on their educational and intellectual calibers and attainments and more so on their economic status. In a rare case, Sri Kala Venkata Rao of Mukkamala was promoted by Nadimpalli Subbaraju of Allavaram – both equidistant to Amalapuram. The patron limited himself to Konaseema, but sent Venkata Rao to the State capital. This economic importance proved itself so useful, so correct and spoke volumes to the judging wisdom of the generous humanist, that he was. Venkatarao rose to the level of Revenue Minister in the Madras Presidency and the National Secretary of Congress.

Since Subbaraju became a great force, he has been eliminated through murder by his party colleagues from the south of Konaseema. They shouted, after the murder, "Inquilab Zindabad" to mislead the public. The entire political atmosphere cannot be described by any one.

Therefore, I just limit myself to some names of places and people.

Because of gross injustices by landlords and money lenders peasantry gradually were drawn to communism. As a liberal variant came the Socialists. Thus, we heard the names of Jayaprakash Narain, PVG Raju and local leader Nalla Reddy Naidu. We have heard of Dange, Gopalan, etc. This place was visited by Sohan Singh Josh, Tejasingh Swatantar, Gopalan etc. Sundarayya and Nagi Reddy are the provincial and Kaneti Mohan Rao, Alluri Venkata Rama Raju, the Konaseema leaders. Mullapudi Suryanarayna penned the history of communist movement in Konaseema.

Almost every village had a communist, a socialist and several congressmen. Most of these became reformers in various fields. Some of these sacrificed their lives - Alluri, Rudraraju, Nanduri, Prerepa, Kandigatla, to mention some names still in memory. Balija community – the peasantry paid most heavy price. Ryali, Yelamanchili Lanka, Korangi, etc became notorious for oppressions of people asking for justice. I have seen how people are prevented from voting. Socially and politically very dynamic and progressive land in those days ! Today? Infos, stories and legends are plenty everywhere.

ORIGIN OF CORRUPTIONS

One of the first initiatives of the government of free India was to benefit the political sufferers who fought for India's freedom. This was done by granting some lands of the government to them. Firstly, the influential people managed to get prime lands not commensurate with their works for the country. By and large all got good lands. More powerful among Congress politicians grabbed these for themselves and useless lands near sea shore and such habitats were exchanged, by force. I knew one such politician of Razole, Lingamurty Raju and several victims, mostly Brahmins, Lands of Antarvedi were given to innocent and gullible people in Konaseema in exchange of good lands, interior. This was later resisted and thus the communist movement was initiated by another, Venkata Rama Raju !

To the best of my memory this constituted the first major corruption pervading the whole country.

In the first elections of 1952, the sympathizers of victims were prevented by three methods – the boats were removed from the islands preventing the dwellers from coming to mainland to vote; people were condemned to the cattle jails and provided liquor and meats for a few days; Lies were spread through wall posters to influence the middle classes. Yet, Konaseema mostly voted for right persons, the communists in the early elections thanks to Malabar Special Police and Rich Congressmen.

JOURNALISM

People here take to reforms easily and enjoy advocacies. Many journalists from this small land flourished - Sihambhatla Jogarao of Blitz, Mahidhara Rama Mohanrao of Visalandhra, Rambhatla Krishna Murty of Eenadu, Ajanta and Ellora of Indian Express, Kagada Sharma to mention a few. The first national award for popularising science came to Nalini Mohana Rao of Munganda. Folk songs of this remote region was collected by Ellora, Godavarti Bhaskara Rao. Gutala Krishna Murty who made a great contribution to English literature from London hails from here. And Kompella Janardhana Rao a comrade of Sri Sri is from Gangalakurru Agrahaaram.

POLITICAL MURDERS AND MANGROVES

During our childhood we occasionally used to see smartly marching Police dragging some one and also find dead bodies moving in water bodies. In fact they are murders, mostly for land, water, crop and justice. There were innumerable cases unrecorded at Korangi police station, off Yanam, opposite Konaseema at the Northern end. And the bodies were thrown into the Mangroves. These shrubby forests begin in the Polavaram Island, from the end of Vrudhagowtami at Kandikuppa, cover the mouth of Gowtami. Korangi, and the other two terminal tributaries and extend north-wards to the south of Kakinada. Korangi Police station became notorious – who ever is taken there is expected to meet a watery grave. Many communists of Konaseema and other nearby parts became food for the aquatic fauna in the mangroves.

NATIONAL RECORD IN MURDERS

National Record in Murders was held by Razole taluka for some years. It outstripped both Kadapa and Fazilka in Punjab. Most murders were agrarian with political contents. Landlords do not part with lands to the tenants; nor do they share the crops with justice. Peasantry was bitter and was embracing communism. Therefore some murders were political. Landlords used to get the prominent peasantry murdered. Interestingly many murders used to take place near the water points and sources or flows. One Lingamurty Raju was credited with most offences – a minister who could not be elected even during Indira Wave! His biggest disappointment was that he could not get his relative Alluri Venkata Rama Raju killed. The latter was an MLA for 5-7 times.

COMMUNIST STORIES

Raju never stayed in one place for long. Often he will stay in the middle of hay-stack, awaiting couriers to bring messages and / or foods. Some comrades learnt how to hold breath for long so as to remain undetected in waters. Kaneti Mohan Rao became famous for climbing trees and jumping from one another. In a famous incident during 1950s, in the region of today's Chinchinada Bridge and Dindee Resort, he escaped the police, climbed the tree and reached the Vasishta banks and escaped into the tall reeds. By the time the police came there he reached the other bank by swimming. Korrapati Pattabhi Ramayya was the most famous person, always in cognito for heroics and escapades.

COMMUNISTS: SEVERAL TYPES

Backgrounds and reasons why one became a

communist differ, not only here, probably everywhere. Since the objective conditions do not change, they do not change. Of course in history many famous personalities did change. Because they had intellectual roots; wanted quick changes; they revolted. One can see some of these cases in the book "THE GOD THAT FAILED" edited by Crossman.

Some are intellectual and doctrinaire. Some are humanistic with genuine concern for the suffering. Some hate injustice. But most are jealous of the well to do. Most belong to the last category. There are some becoming communists because their role models or iconic personalities are communists. They are willing to sacrifice and suffer; eschew comforts of life; honest and unselfish; hard working and helpful.

I am supposed to be a natural communist, who will be eliminated once the party comes to power! because an organised communism is a political animal. To my mind, our ancient society was naturally communistic just as primitive societies everywhere.

BEHAVIOURAL DEVIANTS

Sukanya and Rambabu of Avidi, Subba Rao of Adurru, Manepalli -Kuchi, Jayanti, Bandaru Shanta and a Chaudhari, Razole-Teacher's sex with his own daughter, Khandavilli and Chilaka in Munganda, Kesanakurru's Pallayya Sarma's escapades, Amalapuram's Red-light Areas and Achari and Ramanatha Sarma, are all adventurers, Yerramraju's sodomite exercises with younger and boyish innocents, love affairs, Tata and Ramachandra Rao, Kanakalata and her Suitor, Akondi Gopalam, Tatayya and Chinna Ammamma. The last a kshatriya lady used to stay in the fields of my grand father, landlords' playfulness with underlings. Scattered families of Once-Temple Dancers were sources of juicy gossips in those times.

I came across several abnormal behaviours or conducts, in comparison with predominant mores. They were all therefore secret, some fell into my sights. First was keeping women as wives without marriage. This I saw in Manepalli. Mr. Jayanti from Pedapatnam used to arrive every day at a house distinguished by beauty and music by a mother and daughter. Very near to this house, Mr. Kuchi used to come from Munganda, less frequently than the other-both on distinguished horse carts. Both men are rich Brahmins and both women belonged to the erstwhile Devadasi communities. This was a decadent practice gradually disappeared in the next few decades.

More prevalent, in the place of the above is the illicit sexual relations, clandestinely in the agricultural fields with the working women. These are all escapades of the landlords. The result was the birth of illicit children, in the lower echelons of society, seen often here and there in society, distinguishable!

I heard several students talking of sex for money, the prostitution, at Amalapuram, as back as around late '50s. Stranger were two experiences: First was a brawl in Razole in a teacher's house. I and my classmates passing by heard him shouting down others "She is my daughter, I produced her, just as we eat vegetables, fruits, chick and goats, nurtured by us I use her for sex; what is wrong". We did not understand anything, but reported in our houses. Years later we realised that this incest is not rare but never talked openly.

The strangest was the conduct of a college student at Amalapuram. He simply asks boyish students far younger, to give him company for the night as his parents were out of station. The attendant boy would sleep with him on the same bed as was the practice in all houses in those times. The boy is the object of sodomy somewhere in midnight. Since this was not a daily affair, it continued for long. Almost all boyish students were victims of this misconduct, including me! This has gradually evolved into a permanent feature! How? This rich man became a Yogi, never married, collected donations and established an orphanage for destitute children. Converting sodomy into pedophily is but a small step. He continued this habit for decades as a Swamiji of the Orphanage!

TANTRIC PRACTICES

Occultism is very popular in India from times immemorial. One of its main branches is the worship, propitiaton and wish-fulfilment there of. Tantricism is believed to be mostly useful for negative purposes by its believers. This is supposed to require stout hearts, for working at dead of nights, in graveyards, dealing with all kinds of devils and ferocities and appearances. In Konaseema, this is practised only by some Brahmins and

Muslim Clergy. The town of Nagaram is very famous for this. I have considerable personal experience dealing with them.

HISTORIC ISSUES

These islands have several unique temples with hundreds of years of history. Some of them are in Ryali, Mandapalli, Vanapalli, Ainavilli, Antarvedi, Muramalla. But the most distinguished is the one established by Vyasa Maharshi at Kesanakurru, the last village on Godavari. Despite being the author of Mahabharata and Bhagavadgita there in and a compiler of Vedas, temples for him and by him are rare. I do not know any place with a temple for Veda Vyasa or one built by him.

It is believed that Sanghamitra, the daughter of Ashoka built a Stupa at a village named Adurru [adi + Uru = original village] in the middle island Nagaram! While Adurru represented Buddhist influences, traces of Jain influence were found in Atreyapuram and Nedunuru. Large wells present in some places are considered to indicate this influence. East India Company brought Christianity to these coastal areas.

In Bandarlanka, the finest yarn of 150 counts, used to be produced and woven into fabrics. These were later exported from Bendamoorlanka Port. It was one of the best in India in those times. The factories at this place, and around Yanam and Antarvedi are parts of yore. The Mudunuri Zamindari, Kakarlapudi and Alluri dynasties of this region, also passed into history. River Godavari entering the Bay of Bengal, was described by Viswanatha Satyanarayana as "Cheliyali katta" or a "Union of Girl with her bosom Friend" which now stands corrupted. His another creation, an offering of "Raw Cotton thread to the New Moon [Chandruniko Nulupogu]" with great philosophic under currents, also disappeared from human memory.

ANTARVEDI WASTE LANDS TURNED FERTILE

For decades, may be centuries, pilgrims to Antarvedi temple, and to the confluence point of Godavari with the Bay, for a holy bath, had to wade through saline and marshy soils under hot sun and thurst with no trees or shrubs. Such lands are rare. When Independence came, lands were given to political sufferers. The corrupt local leaders grabbed the good lands and others were given these useless ones. Thus, initiated here was communism, spontaneous resistance, not by Marx or Lenin. Subsequently, these lands were reclaimed by science through a proper management of water and plants, fixation of nitogen and carbon. The unproductive waste lands were reduced to the minimum! A great application of ecology.

BAILEY BRIDGE

Bailey Bridge between Sakhinetipalli and Narsapuram suggested the times to come. Rudraraju Ramalingaraju, aka, Lingamurty Raju, was already notorious for land-related corruptions and their consequences, was a dominant Congress Leader of Konaseema. His son was to marry the daughter of Alluri Satyanarayana Raju of

Chinchinada legacy of Narsapuram. The former was a minister and the latter, the Secretary of the Indian National Congress, after he left the Communist Movement. They are absolute opposites, but brought together by the marital alliance. Two powerful people have brought a bridge through the courtesies of 'the army, for the easy transport of participants in this marriage near Antarvedi! People from all over Konaseema came here just to have a glimpse of the wonder they never imagined. Yet Lingamurty Raju was only feared and never liked. He won the elections only once in many attempts.

SUKANYA, THE MOST GIFTED DEVADASI

That Devadasees have traditionally a cultural role in Konaseema Society is well known. First is to take part in the temple functions. Next is to entertain people during long festivals such as Dussera. During my college days I attended every such function. These Devadasis function in groups of 6-8 leadered by a senior. They are good in dance, music, singing, not necessarily in all and some of them adept in conversations. Rarely one finds knowledgeable people. Sukanya is one such. She was beautiful and good talker, besides her repertoire of craft, dancing. I saw her arguing with many learned audience. Once she was discussing some issues with Burrakatha exponents, Nishtala Brothers of Thanelanka. The whole audience was spell bound with her knowledge. She went to cinemas through Adurti Subba Rao, a famous director. Mullapudi Venkataramana garu told me of her big library, scholarship and gastronomical finesses. But all said, alas, she is treated as a Devadasi. Everyone is not a Subbalakshmi or a Nagarathnamma to get social recognition. The last I heard was that she left for USA and took Adurti Subba Rao along.

Devadasi system may be a pious one, a great one during monarchies, and but ultimately, a cruel one. Studies on this area were very few and fragmentary. Deliverance from the shackles of this system is very difficult. A few Bengalees such as Raja Ram Mohan Roy and Ishwar Chandra Vidya Sagar and a few Telugus, Gurajada Appa Rao and Veeresalingam, Maharaja of Mysore worked to change the system or humanize. Very few successes. Others such as Nagaratnamma from Mysore, Subbalaxmi and Paramasivam from Madurai, Jayanti Pantulu from Pedapatnam, Adurti Subba Rao and Nidamarty Durgayya Sastry from Rajahmundry and many more did attempt to liberate them and protect the liberated.

Injustice anywhere, in any form, must be prevented. This used to be my most dominant desire to pursue, but did not succeed much.

MISCELLANY

THE FAMOUS POLASA FISH OF VASISHTA

This is the most celebrated of the germplasms of this region, the other being the Ganga Bondam of Bendamoorlanka. **So many Islands and so many name Sakes:** There are several villages christened with "Lanka" as the suffix, although not an island. Similarly there are many Islands with small populations in all the riverine water bodies. Beach sand quality different from others: Sand in the local beaches is small and whiter which gave an agreeable quality to it. This is an area needing researches.

DRAINAGE IN DELTA SYSTEMS

Deltas rich in river waters which aid in extensive cropping could suffer water-logging if rains too are high. Therefore a special drainage system, in the form of canals was formed here to decant all excessive water. Often these are used for navigation. Something strange and common in this delta are the illegitimate children, mostly consummated to the landlords and labourers in the huts maintained in the fields. Landlords take care of the kids and the ill-wed mothers keep quiet about the episodes. The caste elite have constructed hostels for the children of their castes. One of the famous was the one built by Sirangu Sattiraju of Vilasavilli. Many Kapus did the same under the influence of the socialist leader Nalla Reddy Naidu.

The land is full of temples and trees – Banyan being the most iconic. The Banyan in the Elaminchili lanka, opposite Sivakodu, was infamous for police murders of alleged communists. Konaseema is also famous for beautifully maintained tanks storing Godavari water for mostly drinking purposes. Some villages have more than one. A temple on the banks normally protects the tank's health. Choultrys for passengers in important places is a custom in Godavari districts. From this land of waters, came the great maestro, Mangalampalli, Philosophers such as some Sankaracharyas and Swamis and a great journalist, Rambhatla Krishna Murty. The last was a close friend of Eenadu's Ramoji Rao and trained most of the journalist force under them. Probably they alone address each other in monosyllables!

PORA, A UNIQUE ECOSYSTEM THREATENED

It appears that Mangrove ecosystem of Godavari river originated in the Katrenikona Mandal, continued through Polavaram Mandal, traversed the entry point of Gautami into Bay of Bengal at Bhairava Palem. Later they got into the Koringa complex of waters to constitute the Sanctuary to cater to the pleasures of tourists and coffers of the government!

50 years ago Pandi and Pora were the bigger mounds supporting several houses each while most supported not more than 3. All these could be seen on way to Sacramento Light House from Kandikuppa [kanthi = Sea, Krupa= Mercy] on boats in the forenoon or by foot in the evening, on retreat. Each mound owned one to three boats for transport. Gradually some mounds expanded with deposits, mergers, people and mangroves - all for each other. Pora got a road on one side to connect with the main road. A few dozens became a few thousands of people obtaining commons such as education, health and transport.

A danger, Damocles sword, looms on the entire ecosystem. I am informed of cutting off of mangroves and give this improper soil for housing to the poor families. Such non-local people become the origins of social problems through conversions to Christianity adding to ecological problems. This ecosystem bore countless cyclones, floods and atleast 2 Uppenas [Sunamis], but unlikely to survive this politically designed slaughter of environment and society. A 250 sq. km mangrove continuity from Polavaram Island originated from river waters of Godavari, but extended beyond into a WILDLIFE SANCTUARY AT YANAM. Without Konaseema and Godavari, no mangroves would have formed or survived any where north, for tourism.

RESEARCH INPUTS

All said, blanks are glaring. Enormous research inputs are necessary - geological and ecological from Antarvedi to Kakinada into all aspects. This must cover a length shelf through beach waters upto 10-20 km interior into the land from continental. Researcher Seshgiri Rao, did not continue Palynology. M. Suryanarayana's work on Marakallu was not continued after his retirement. Fishermen and boatmen of the coast and the Mangroves, Marakallu – their lineage from the Maricars of Karaikal – their descent from the Arabic Migrants and Moplas need to be studid. Some work from Madras University was to be followed up. The entire stretch from Antarvedi to Kakinada should be a Research Site.

FEATS AND FANTACIES

We frequently saw fantastic feats performed by some nomadic families – a mix of gymnastics, circus feats, animal controlling etc. We never understood but enjoyed. We never knew how some people pull boats with ropes for long distances, how some others could carry palanquins on shoulders and walk for long [Uppada], how some could wade through waters fully sunk and search underneath [konaseema coast] and how some used to catch snakes easily, and charm them when most dread them!

BRAHMN HATRED

In Devadasi societies, as the Rajas changed gradually - the rich society took over them - Jamindars, Temple Trustees, etc. Some Devadasis, on the sly, used to maintain romantic relationships with Brahmins with talents for the sake of superior progenies. This dichotomy between relations for money and relations for progenies gradually developed into hatreds towards the secret donors of desired genes. These scenarios ramified in time. Such that the original causes of hatred were obscured. But this is the origin. In every part where Devadasis were considerable, one can discern the hatred of rich non-Brahmins towards the Brahmins, apparently for no reason !

Among the educated non-Brahmins there was universal resentment for keeping them away from traditional higher learning. In Tamilnadu with whom Andhra coexisted for long, it is added by job competition and orthodox conducts towards the lower castes. Reasons for hatred differed from place to place.

Fig. 5: Waters from the Koringa Complex entering the Bay of Bengal through Several Streams.

Fig. 6: Waters from the Koringa Complex entering the Bay of Bengal -A Platform for tourists and Mechanised Boats.

Fig. 7: Pallam, an exemplary Village, surrounded by water on all sides.

Fig. 8: Buddhist Archeological Remains at a Village called Adurru.

Fig. 9: A Festival of People with their favourite Gods–Prabhala Teertham.

Fig. 10: Meeting Point of sea and a channel of Godavari beyond Yanam, showing two boats.

Fig. 11: A typical Ferry Scene anywhere in Konaseema.

Fig. 12: Narasimha Temple at Antarvedi between River and Sea.

CHAPTER - 2

CHILDHOOD

Independence Day

Kadapa

the first Sojurn

Kadapa Kotireddy, Ramasubbamma, Kala Venkata Rao and Sitaramayya, my grand father,

Vakatippa

My father's Native Place

Raja of Ramachandrapuram

Ingratitude of some families

Grand father's madness or discipline

Kesanakurru

My Mother's Native Place

Newspaper in the daily life

Floods of 1953

Immigration of six families –

Island Kavulu - Ramasastry

Durgayya and Kishtamma – two titans

Island Polavaram

Karma Yogam and Purushottamaprapti Yogam

Routhu Sitaramayya, an all purpose man

INDEPENDENCE DAY

Childhood is the best part of any one's life. Unfortunately most of it is not remembered. Grand parents tell our tales. My own memory was awakening probably around the time of India's independence. I remember chewing peppermint wearing white shirts tucked in khaki knickers, with white caps. Festoons everywhere. Children are made to march in the main streets singing patriotic songs. Yes it was the beginning of new slavery to our local chieftains in the name of freedom that actually never came even now. I was at Kesanakurru, my mothers home, on Vrudhagoutami.

This freedom did not come to my father's place, Vakatippa on Gautami, 8 miles from Ramachandrapuram. It took place at Polavaram where my father was posted as a supervisor of the SKCC Bank, the scene was different. There was celebration. The local landlord – Buchi Krishnam Raju was a Congress leader. There was a long row of Bullock Carts, very decorated, leaders of all hues in white dress and white cap, named Gandhi cap; singing patriotic songs; distributing sweets to one and all. Only the landed gentry celebrated the transfer of power to India, to themselves.

I was a mere 4+ of age! Since the whole land mass was an island, the village used to be called Island Polavaram.

KADAPA, the First Sojurn

It was an adventure- for my father and mother, the brief sojourn at Kadapa; on account of my father's job there for less than a year, his maiden one. The job was offered by the then minister in Rajaji's cabinet, Kotireddy a major Congress leader of those times and a friend of my grand father in Congress Sevadal. In a chance meeting, the minister enquired from my grand father what his son was doing. Finding him job-less and qualified, he asked him to send him there. My father joined his first job in the Rayalaseema Co-operative Bank at Kadapa. This is how we were there.

WANDER LUST

I was ceased by a kind of wander lust at that age. It was very difficult for my mother to control my wanderings. In one occasion, I disappeared on a forenoon from the vicinity of the house. There was a commotion among local people that sent neighbours and friends in search of me. Just before dusk an affluent Reddy family brought me home. They told that I strayed into their courtyard by chance, nearby. The women folk were enamoured by my then ways, gave biscuits while I continued to entertain them through pranks and tantrums. After enjoying sumptuous milk and biscuits, I went to sleep. After waking up, I was brought to my house. Ever since, my excursions to their house became regular, and eating biscuits too!

GADDI BAZAAR, FALLING FROM TERRACE

In Kadapa, we were living in Gaddi [Hay, Grass] Bazaar. There was an incidents narrated by my parents. Once I was playing on the terrace of the house along with other children, flying kites. Accidentally I fell down from the parapet! Every one was shouting, screaming and crying. I was taken for wounded. All came down to collect my battered body with broken limbs. Lo and behold, as they came to gather me, I came out with smiles and ran towards them. I fell on the haystack.

KADAPA KOTIREDDY, RAMASUBBAMMA, KALA VENKATA RAO AND SITARAMAYYA, MY GRAND FATHER

My paternal grand father, Sitaramayya and Koti Reddy were among the ADCs assigned to the Congress President, P C Ray, for the Annual Session at Cocanada. Prof. Ray was a visionary and instrumental in establishing the famous "Bengal Chemicals" and later "Bengal Lamps". That economic improvement of people is very important, and has to go along with political independence was ignored by most national leaders. Perhaps only Dadabhai Naoroji, Ambedkar and T. Prakasam thought in these lines. Ray often used to comment when asked about his bachelorhood "*I married my chemistry*" – my grand father used to quote.

Kadapa Kotireddy and his wife Rama Subbamma were among the very important leaders of those Ceded districts, in those days and respected all over the Madras Presidency. But this was not to continue for long. One day, another minister of Rajaji's cabinet, Kala Venkata Rao, happened to see my grand father. On enquiry he found that my father is in Kadapa. He was annoyed "when I am here why do you send your son so far away. Ask him join the Konaseema Co-operative Central Bank at Amalapuram". The bank posted my father at Island Polavaram.

Their friendship continued for years. Goodness and honesty were the bases. On the other hand, Kala Venkata Rao of Amalapuram and my grand father were college mates at Rajahmundry. Their other close friends were Mallipudi Pallam Raju of Cocanada, Bikkini Venkata Ratnam of Ramachandrapuram and Narasimhadevara Satyanarayana of Alamuru. All these became important leaders and obtained some positions. My grand father became a pauper, selling his properties mostly for financing these people during freedom movement. Kala Venkata Rao only provided a small job in a competitive spirit with Kotireddy! But he was peerless!

We are back at the ecosystem where we belonged, I. Polavaram. My childhood was mostly spent here for nearly 7 years and in Kesanakurru, an adjacent village and a native place of my mother. Before we deal with these two villages, a note on my father's native place, Vakatippa.

VAKATIPPA, Our Ancestral Native Place

I do not know for how many generations this village has been our native place. By the time I developed some memory we are in a cocoanut grove nearly of one acre. My great grand father, Ramachandrudu was given this grove and adjacent rice fields of 18 acres as gift by the Raja of Ramachandrapuram for services rendered. There was and is a water supply channel in between rice and cocoanut fields. He built a house, one of the best in those days in that village just opposite this grove. Through very crooked means this was usurped by a relative from my grand father. It is alive even today in the hands of that unethical family.

My life was limited to this grove that has seen many vicissitudes of life – good things, bad things, cheating, exploitation and hood winking, what not! We lost all by the time I became 5-years old. This was in short a social commentary on Brahmins becoming decadent and hypocrites.

RAJA OF RAMACHANDRAPURAM AND VAKATIPPA

This dynasty owned huge lands covering several villages surrounding the temple of Bheemeswara in Draksharama. This raja was an actual brother of Raja of Island Polavaram, adopted by Kota Ramachandrapuram. My grand father's father Ramachandrudu garu was his employee. Pleased with his services, the rajah presented him a cocoanut Grove and 17 acres of Rice field adjacent to it with a water channel originating from Cotton's Barrage. This did not remain for long and lost before the grand children came of age.

The simplicity or foolishness, idealism or stupidity of my grand father was legendary and must be seen to believe. It was lost due to his spending ways on friends in the freedom movement [Kala, Mallipudi, Venkataratnam, Narasimhadevara etc] or by a relative, Geddam family – Sarveswara Rao through endless cheating or by his brother-in-law – Mahidhara Kameswara Rao who used to leave his family of 8-10 people every year on him for 3 months like a swarm of locusts. This continued for over a decade. Net result is a pauperisation. But the great house remains even now occupied by the Geddam family's latest generations.

A wiseacre remarked. This wealth was obtained by laisioning between Mandapeta Devadasis and the Raja. So it has to go only this way! And the Geddam family were Dance and Music teachers of the Mandapeta Devadasis, for long. Mandapeta in those times was no less than Tanjavur.

INGRATITUDE OF SOME FAMILIES

BIKKINI FAMILY

This migrant family first ingratiated themselves to my grand father and his mother through their relatives living in front of our cocoanut grove. These relatives were our friends for decades before and after. By telling sob stories and telling imaginary and false difficulties they won the sympathies of my grand father. All these centered around their dwelling vagaries. In a weaker movement, my grand father allowed them to put a hut in one corner. They chose the corner nearest to the road! As he is often out of station they have expanded it with the approval of my great grand mother.

The structure was damaged due to heavy rains and sought the permission of my grand father to repair. Lo and Behold, they made a brick house and the thatching is replaced by tiles! On enquiry he defended saying, "gales keep on destroying, therefore this permanent structure because you will not object being our benefactor". Some time later, when in Rajahmundry, he met my grandfather along with some more friends, to donate that little land to him, as he is a good man. At last they offered a price, but not disclosed. They took him to the Registrar's office, and made him sign the documents. When asked for the price, they said "we should not take anything free from a Brahmin, therefore we give you Rs 116."

After a few days, a boundary wall came up. There was a quarrel and shoutings. He brought there the village leadership and showed the registration documents. The wall is within the dimensions mentioned in the Document! Regular quarrels used to happen around this wall, as they would throw egg shells, bones etc into our grove. This is the saga of a well planned and executed treachery for gain.

Fifty years later, I met a college lecturer at Patiala. We were talking on Phone. On enquiry, he found I am the grandson of the man cheated continuously by his grand father. At once he put down the phone and never spoke again. What his grand father must have told. Even today that family is not trusted in the village by his own caste people!

GEDDAM FAMILY

After my retirement I went to see my native village. By chance, I landed in front of this very Cocoanut Grove where in we lived in my childhood. The opposite house had some people in the veranda. They enquired of me and at once they invited me saying that "This was your own house". That was a huge strong house of my grand father, built by his father, but lost to a relative, Geddam Sarveswara Rao, due to his chicanery. The man who invited me into the house was the last son of this hoodwinker relative. One of the best houses of the village built inlate 1930s, still in tact in 2015, was usurped by this man who was trusted by my then family. The story goes like this.

My grand father was married to an impossible and illiterate lady, despite his opposition, by his mother. He had no contentment at all from the family. This was made use of by Mr. Geddam! He was drawn astray towards Devadasi concubines. Geddam's families were Natyacharyas, mostly teaching to temple dancers, devadasis, who were in large numbers in towns such as Mandapeta, Rajahmundry, etc. Therefore, he used to have acquaintance with most of them. My grand father was enticed to one he was enamoured of. The errands became more serious while he was still a student in Rajahmundry. At a weaker moment, he was lured to register his house as a gift to her, just a "fake". Because she would never come to the village! In reality it was registered in Geddam's name! Gradually we were cajoled to move into the grove, opposite, where he himself built a large hut, and praised that Sitaramayya is now exactly living like Gandhi, his hero! As long as our family lived there, this Geddam Sarveswaa Rao black mailed him, holding Devadasi secrets. When we left this village for Polavaram, he took away all furniture- of teakwood – made in advance for his future legal profession, which never materialised!

MAHIDHARA FAMILY

This family head, Kameswara Rao was the brother-in-law of my grand father. He had eight children, the last two being girls. He was a middle school teacher and later a Head Master. As soon as the summer holidays are declared, the entire family of nearly ten will descend on this Home in the cocoanut grove, i.e. during the last week of March. They will remain here until the middle of June, an entire 3 month period. This has probably began as a courtesy, then tradition, later became a design amd turned into blackmail!

Their intention was to escape from the living expenditure for this period. My grand father simply fulfils the desire of his mother for her only daughter! There was another unspoken aspect. My grand father had 3 daughters by his second marriage; his brother-in-law had 6 sons. He hoped to arrange his daughters' marriages with some of them! The second marriage, its history, progress and aftermath was a topic of epic proportions for any writer! Thus, there are three concerns - The Grove, The Second Marriage of my grand father, and the summer Blackmail of his own Brother-in-law.

I am concerned with the first. The second and third, that plagued our family for half a century are of interest to a Munshi Prem Chand or a Sarat Chandra Chatterjee or a Jane Austen.

The grove was unforgettable. It is of about one acre. The grove has, a water channel at one side and a road on the other. In between, at the central part and nearer to the road, a large thatched house was constructed, after the Geddam has usurped our big cemented house with an open square at the centre. The house has a Cocoanut tree at the centre and a Sapota tree at the edge. Along the channel were two rhizomatous herbs in large numbers, used as vegetables. In one corner bananas and plantains were cultivated. At the other end was an orange tree. In one corner Acacia trees with small yellow flowers were cultivated, a great rarity in those days, but a common sight at the shorelines of most tanks in Tamil Nadu. These were meant to supply fuel wood in rainy season. All over the areas are a variety of herbs growing spontaneously, used as vegetables and as medicines. The cows are tied to the cocoanut trees randomly. The Bikkini family usurped about 1000 sq.ft. and made a habit of throwing wastes into our garden. Showing enmity, building it or provoking it, is natural with all ingrates feigning in justice falsely!

THREE WOMEN

My grand father frittered away everything and had no place even to place the teak wood furniture made for his future legal profession, and a large number of books. Everyone took them away and so his furniture. All life, he suffered due to his mother, his wife, his sister and her entire family of leeches, his generosity, his inherent foolishness, utopian thinking and absence of managerial ability.

He was left with nothing but derision. The two books he left for me were always kept with some pride - one was the original edition of Geetanjali by Tagore and the second is a Fundamental book on Botany. Even in those times and life he was a sad failure. I always have a considerate feeling for him. For he was a good man, naïve, patriotic and gullible - some of the qualities I inherited through my father, and similarly suffering.

GRAND FATHER'S MADNESS OR DISCIPLINE

When my father was working in Razole, he took all of us to a pilgrimage at Antarvedi at the confluence of Vashistha river and the Bay of Bengal, on an auspicious day. Some neighbours too accompanied. The next day, my father fell ill and has fallen on the road itself very near to the temple. All were watching the spectacle, mother, myself and my two brothers. All of a sudden a gentleman came watched my father for a while and exclaimed loudly "are you Ramachandram from Vakatippa?" and said further I am your classmate Sundara Sivudu. I used to take food in your house. We used to go to the High School together. My father became normal and they exchanged lots of informations.

The stranger then told to all around, the following story. Sivudu, Ramachandram and the son of Katta Venkanna, the Share Cropper, were classmates educated by my grand father, the landlord. In the SSLC final my father passed but with low Marks. In anger, He paid the fees for the other two boys to continue in the college, and admitted my father in a Co-Operative Training

Institute. When confronted, he justified this as this is a part of Gandhian Movement, which advocated the Philosophy of co-operation in all fields! Sivudu was then the Tahasildar, assured us all help whenever we want and left reluctantly.

SECOND MARRIAGE OF "STUPID SITARAMAYYA"

He was vexed with his mother and her confidantes, but mothers cannot be changed. He was much harassed by his wife, my grand mother. Since he had no conjugal life at all, what to talk of bliss, his brother-in-law with the consent of his mother married him again. The girl was 9 years old then and has to wait for her maturity for over 5 years. This naiveté earned him a prefix "Stupid Sitaramayya". He should have married one, atleast 10 years, older!

"GOAT MILK SITARAMAYYA"

After my birth, my mother had no milk to feed. On trial and error goat milk was found suitable to my physiology. Some goats were maintained in the grove. The village made fun of him as a true follower of Gandhi!

GROVE-TOURISM WITH MARIDI, THE HARIJAN

There used to be a Harijan by name Maridi, in the service of my grand father. His work was to look after the entire grove. He just wore a loin cloth and another smaller cloth around his head. For some unknown reason

I became fond of him, and he, of me. In those days Dalits were not allowed to touch upper caste children. But I was allowed. Whenever I see him, I run to him and climb to sit on his shoulder, holding his head with both of my hands, a strong embrace. He would then take me around the grove. Other children similarly enjoyed this tourist facility. The whole village just laughed away, in shock. "Oh! This stupid Sitaramayya is a Gandhi follower". The other man who would similarly take me around was Jabbu Tata the sickly grandfather. He was the youngest brother of the father of my grandfather. Viswanatham was mentally unsteady and unmarried.

From here we moved to Polavaram and thus to Kesanakurru, 2 miles away and that much nearer to Godavari river. These two villages and child hood never left me. The period in my life was such. I was always moving between these villages at will, and as I fancied, often without telling any one. My prodigality, pranks and tantrums were always a source of worries and concern to all the concerned albeit temporary but a perennial headache.

My grand father had
everything, and nothing.
He allowed others to plunder him,
but he kept smiling.
He was very unfortunate
but remained a fool
He learned nothing
And forgot nothing
I seem to be true inheritor of him!

KESANAKURRU, My Mother's Native Place

Kesanakurru is the last village on the course of Godavari. Godavari divides into Vasishta and Gautami tributaries. From Gautami another minor tributary parts just before coursing into Yanam and thence into the sea through several channels like Koringa. This is Vrudha Gautami. The last village on it was Kesanakurru on the left side, before subdividing and meeting the sea through mangroves. There was at the terminus a light house. This ecosystem is unique by itself. Today there is an extension to Kesanakurru, the Palem.

In those days this village was famous for a particular variety of Capsicum, long and bright red, mostly cultivated on the Godavari banks or flood plains, between the Embankments and the shoreline. Also famous are variety of insect – resistant cocoanut and mini- Mangoe. One such tree is still alive and productive even now!

The only temple by Vyasa Maharshi in Telugu-speaking country, probably the whole South India is in this village, a uniqueness in itself. Besides the river, it has a canal and a well kept tank. The other by him is in Kasi on Ganga.

Kesanakurru suddenly became famous in 1952 due to a Music Band. Earlier people had to go towards Yanam and Kakinada or Mummidivaram and Amalapuram for getting musicians for every function – personal or social or divine. The youngsters of Barber Community from Kesanakurru formed a band useful for the island. It is another story that most of them perished in the

Cholera epidemic that invaded the island following the 1953 floods.

An interesting social aspect is the population, neighbours and relationships. Very near to the village tank there happened to be four beautiful girls/ladies from the road nearest to the tank. Venkatalakshmi, Durgayya Sastry's daughter Swarajyalakshmi and Radha, 2 sisters related to Sastriji and a 4th one Bhanumati, daughter of Kishtamma garu. These four are very fair, more or less of similar built and beautiful.

Venkata Lakshmi, called Chitti, had children slightly elder to the children of the other three. Incidentally these children were childhood friends too. A very strange kinship between some of them dated from August 15th, 1947. She brooded a large family of very talented children. A parallel to her family from Munganda is indeed rare.

COMMUNISTIC PRANKS OF MY UNCLE

My uncle, my mother's younger brother and the last child of my grand parents was a regular headache to my grand father. He studied until 5th standard and did not go to high school. He was under communist influence. He gets regularly Soviet Land in Telugu. And almost maintained a library of some books, obtained free from some sources. The value of books and libraries stuck with me all life!

He would put the communist flag on the top of the house and enjoys its fluttering as if communism has come to his place. On the walls of his own house he painted hammer and sickle. Whenever the police came to our village my grand father had a hectic time in white washing the walls and removing the red flag from the house top. This was used to be a regular game.

Once the Reserve [Malabar] Police mistakenly entered our house and confiscated the rice bags lying on a table. Some one misled them that my grand father was a landlord and had a rich harvest. The fact was just opposite. Exhibiting political sympathies by weaker persons adds to their miseries! Having lost the rice, we had to struggle a good deal, to buy them afresh.

NEWSPAPER IN THE DAILY LIFE

Ours was one of the few houses receiving the newspaper in Telugu. Every day in the morning several people under the leadership of the village Munsif, Akkala Satti Raju, gather in the outer veranda of our house and my grand father will read the headlines. Who ever was interested in a particular news, he used to explain. Any questions from the gathering are also answered by him with analysis. During this time I used to sit on his lap.

When Stalin died, I never understood his commentary, but I ran inside the house and told my grand mother that Stalin died. She at once asked of his village and family. I returned to the gathering in the veranda asking the same question. There were loud guffaws of laughter! The importance of Newspapers never left my system!

FLOODS OF 1953

Godavari Floods of 1953 ended my childhood and its sweetness. These were very devastating. Properties lost. People died in large numbers. Cattle and whole houses were swept. A lot more died due to infectious disease such as cholera. The whole island was in waters except Polavaram and Kesanakurru. SKCC bank reshuffled all its supervisors. Thus, my father was transferred from this northern end to Manepalli village in the southern island. I entered a new school, a high school.

CULTURE

I was introduced here to both culture as well as reforms. I enjoyed and later became a fan of Harikatha, Burra katha, Puppetry, Violin Concerts by very famous people. My grand father was always the chief organiser.

FRIENDS

Among my bosom friends here are Babi, grand son of Durgayya Sastri, Chitti, son of Goda Abbulu. Satyam, son of Karra Pallayya. There would be occasional visitors, such as Datla Brothers. We roam about the tank, the canal, the banyan tree, make and play fans with the leaves of Toddy Palm and thorns of gum tree against winds, make minitoys, tops from the special clay from the river. Durgayya Tata was a titan among scholars. Karras were miserly and self-centered. Babi and me were the closest – we participated in the celebrations on 1947 August 15. Our friendship lasted until my father was transferred to

Razole area. The last outing we had was to roam on the embankments of Godavari during floods during August of 1953.

IMMIGRATION OF SIX FAMILIES- ISLAND KAVULU - RAMASASTRY

Incidentally two historical episodes come to my mind here. And both are inter-related. This island has seen famines and floods alternately for decades. So too human migrations and immigrations. One of the last immigrations saw six brahmin families coming here from Vijayanagaram region, led by the most learned among them the Merusomayajula family. Others were Mahidhara, Gudimetla, Saraswatula, Pulle and Susarla. In these families there used to be several poets – known then as “Island Kavulu”. Before these, one Ramasastry from Saraswatula family wrote Ramayanam - of his brand! Merusomayajula was originally Merubhatla, until an ancestor performed a Yagna.

REFORMS OF KISHTAMMA, MY GRAND FATHER

My grand father believed in change. Culture will be lost if not reformed and especially if not open to all. He practiced. Even today he is remembered in many villages of this region as a reformist, by the Brahmins. He maintained that Brahmins must reform themselves – others will follow. He invited and provided a separate sitting place in all events to the lower and untouchable classes, forbidden from these festivities in those times.

My grand father used to be referred to as "Kishtamma", Amma of Krishna out of sheer affection, admiration and his skills in many fields and always good and smiling to all. He was not Karnam, not Panchayat President, not Village Munsif, not a Teacher, not a Pandit, not a Doctor, not a Purohit, not an Astrologer. But a Farmer and House Holder. Yet he wielded so much popularity. He was trusted by people. A very great character in my life.

In the evenings he used to narrate to the women folk of lower castes in their locality, in the house of the village Munsif, Akkala Sattiraju, Ramayanam, Mahabharatam and Bhagavatam. When Brahmins opposed him near the sacred tank, he confronted them successfully as he was unbeatable in Tarkam, and left the Tank for ever. He would daily go to the River and complete his ablutions before sun rise. Except doing Suryanamaskarams, I have never seen him going to any temple. My grand mother was never doing a daily prayer except to the sacred Tulasi Plant around Sunrise. He sent me to the colony of Untouchables, along with his youngest son, my uncle in Polavaram to tell them hygiene and sanitation, and encourage them to go to school.

The importance I got by those people
I never got again from any where.
The lessons I got from the above
were never forgotten.

DURGAYYA AND KISHTAMMA – TWO TITANS

Durgayya Sastri is the grand father of my friend Babi. I also called him and his brother Venkanna, Tatas. They are scholars. They are poets and interpreters of Sastras. All villagers go to them for any advice or guidelines and respected universally. Both were impoverished due to various reasons. Venkanna Sastri was a Bhagavatar, a reputed harikatha exponent.

Why do I bring them here. Yes I have an intention. Most villages in Konaseema have Brahmins and priests – both knowledgeable. Every village has atleast two such contrasting Brahmins. A rarity and responsible for predominantly reformistic, socialistic, communistic, and agnostic trends in Coastal Andhra leadered by Brahmins.

The village has a sizable population of Brahmins from mostly 4 diferent sub-sects. These two stalwarts do not belong to the major sects, yet they wield greater influence than their numbers or wealth allowed! Durgayya Tata often chided Kishtamma Tata for corrupting traditions. What did he do? He was teaching Puranas to the community of Village Munsif, a Kapu, Akkala Sattiraju. Another sin was; he was allowing the untouchables to cultural festivities such as Harikatha, or Musical festivities. Because of this Kishtamma was liked by these communities, considered a reformist, and Kshatriyas adored the erudition of Durgayya Sastry. And these two rarely used to meet!

A few words at last about Vyasakasi and Kandi Kuppa Kesanakurru was derived from a request in Sanskrit "Kasi Na Kuru" meaning "Do not make this into Kashi". Similarly Kandi Kuppa is a corruption of "Kanthi Krupa" meaning at the mercy of Sea. Truly this village could not have suvived the onslought of marine waves but for providential forces!

POLAVARAM, and SICKNESSES

Due to my father's job we landed in Polavaram. We continued here for 6 years until 1953. I was in 8th standard or 3rd Form. This period probably was my happiest time. For every one childhood is the best time.

Most of the time I used to be ill on account of some thing or the other. Fever is the common one. How is it cured? Starving for 3, 5, 7 days followed by careful eating for some weeks! Many a time I used to be injured due to my pranks. Running and falling, ending up in scratches. Village level plays, Cigarette Packs, Marbles, etc Hide and Seek, mostly with the lower castes, usually left me with some minor wounds very often.

Once I seriously fell ill. My hands as well as legs are out of control at joints. I had to be carried to the Doctor's house. They would dress with a new dose of external medicine around the joints. This medicine was made by them with the base of terminal buds of cocoanut and date palms. Once the terminal bud is gone the tree becomes useless. That was the cost of this medicine. This was rheumatoid arthritis. Akondis sacrificed their own trees more than twice!

There is only one doctor-family for the entire island - The Akondi Ramamurty family. I was the most frequent patient to them. His eldest son Rajagopalam, grand son Satyam were later joined by some other relatives. Some medicines are made by them. Some are brought from Chintaluru, a close by village to Vakatippa, my native place. Their tradition still continues.

CAMARADERIE WITH LOWER CASTES

I had greater camaraderie with lower caste children, going with them on errands to riverside, canals, fields, tanks with buffaloes etc. I was beaten many times, yet I am always attracted to their groups.

Picking up empty match boxes, cigarette packets, thrown butts of cigarettes and beedis used to be a hobby among us, the children. The former was to play with and the latter to try smoking them.

I used to be far away from anything related to education. Schools and teachers were alien to me. But what my mother used to tell, I was listening with great sincerity. It used to be a frequent sight in the village when able-bodied senior students carry me to school using an art of twisting arms to hold me and carry through the village! Akondi Boys-Ramam etc, Mangipudi Brothers, Annapantula Brothers, Nissankula Raja Rao and Venkayya and his cousins were all among my friends.

SUBBAMMA'S DOG

Once friends challenged me to run and jump over a resting dog. I did but he chased me and bitten me. This dog was our pet dog of all in the street. He used to sleep with cats. His host Subbamma reared both dogs and cats. She always sleeps in the cot with them on each side of her body. She is a legend of the village – having no husband and relatives. Only the dogs and cats.

My mother, a classical singer used to teach neighbouring girls Ashtapadis, Tyagaraja Kirtanas and Tarangams. My duty was to carefully write them for the girls. Some of those girls are still alive in Today's Polavaram. Every day in the evening, my mother used to pray. I used to sit with her. The prayer used to change periodically. After some time I had to do the prayer from the book and loudly. Thus, Krishna Satakam and Bhagavat Gita, were recited daily and most of them were remembered for long.

Music-oral and instrumental, traditional performing arts, Prayers-no one was exposed to so many and so much, in both these villages before and after. That was my great privilege.

AKONDI FAMILY

This Akondi family was famous for other than medicine. – Education, Knowledge, Culture, Literary activities and good manners. Getting accepted and entering their house itself is a privilege. I was singularly lucky to be among their favourites. Some very eminent writers in Andhra are their very close relatives.

MAIN STREET OF POLAVARAM

We were staying in the main street of the village in the house of Vysyas. No Brahmin house was available. The first house and the second houses belonged to the Rajahs, Zamindars of the village Achibabu and

Chittibabu. The third house is of Akondi Family. A few more houses belonged to Brahmins. And then the Vysya Houses. The village elementary School, following this is a Muslim colony and a mosque. After a distance is the Malapalli, belonging to Scheduled Castes. Then comes the Irrigation channel.

By any account this is a unique street. All temple festivities move through this street. All mosque festivities also. So too are the traditions of the village Protector-Deity-Pochalamma from the first to the last house – covering Brahmins, Kshatriyas, Vysyas, Kapus, Muslims and the Dalits! All in a fraternal atmosphere.

MOHARRAM

During Moharram, when the "peers" pass in front of my house the near by women and my mother offered, year after year, camphor, incense sticks, vermilion and turmeric in a typically universal Hindu way. The mulla blessed us all.

A HATER OF MOTHER

He is on a bed in the outer area of the house. He is expected to die any moment. The wife took a last look. The son yelled at her. She moved out; went to the backside of house; moved fast along the fields; reached the village tank and jumped into the well nearby. By the time people realised and took out her, she is dead long ago. She was my grand mother' cousin; Saraswatula Rama Murty's mother; considered the kindest women in that area who did not want to live as a widow. Her husband was a tyrant always abusing her. Imitating this habit his only son also continued the same but with the mother. He was a small time freedom fighter spending his wealth. He hated the mother for moralising as it is the wont with all mothers. Then he will rebuke her like his father before, and threaten to punish her once she becomes a widow. One of his threats, was "I will get your head shaven every week and make razor wounds" I have not heard or read about such conducts anywhere and any time.

ACHHIBABU, THE GOOD AND THE BRAVE

The first house on this street is a small palace or a big bungalow. In front of the house is a big Banyan tree. As one enters the building there is a huge garden of a great variety of plants. From the centre passes a narrow verandah lined by cages of birds. One is a mini-botanical garden and another mini-zoo. These two are the hobbies of the owner Zamindar, Raja Kakarlapudi Achyuta Rama Raju, popularly called to as Achhibabu. He is liked by the whole village.

CRICKET

The most unique and memorable experience with him was Cricket. This is rather unbelievable, for it was in early 1950's and in a remote village, where there is only an elementary school. Every day in the afternoon around 4 pm we take all paraphernalia from his house to a near by ground, similar to a stadium. Wickets, Mats, Pads, Balls and Bats all in place. We children are mostly used for fielding. He used to give batting chance to all of us in the beginning and at the end. Barring his older cronies, children will be about half-a-dozen – his children, Akondi children and me.

HUNTING, AVIARY AND THE GARDEN

In front of his house on the other side there is a large vacant ground. Every evening as the birds return to their homes, he practices shooting them. Only a few are hit. The birds become a part of the dinner. He is also an expert in catching snakes. I saw once he held a cobra upside down and hit on the Banyan tree to death. I, had an entry into his palace too to play with his two sons and daughter.

Achhibabu was a great Hunter. He occasionally uses to go for hunting in the forests. His trophies include wild animals such as Pigs and Bucks, brought by him. They were consumed in an open feast by all his assistants, servants and some invitees.

In the front yard of his palace, a big garden was maintained. And on the pavements, an aviary. The former supported a great variety of flowering plants, mostly shrubs and herbs, and the latter of very colourful and singing birds. Individually no one is allowed to enter this place. There were exceptions, I enjoyed this privilege. Every day I used to come to his palace and collect a variety of flowers, in small numbers, in a special silver carriage. These were meant for the daily offerings to God, so well described by Tagore in his Geetanjali!

ELECTIONS OF 1952 AND TANGUTURI PRAKASAM

With such a man I had a confrontation. I was recklessly bold with him, due to ignorance and innocence. This has endeared me to him. It was 1952 elections. There was a small split in the Congress party. The rebels, called Praja Party was contesting from our constituency, Amalapuram. The Congress candidate was Kala Venkata Rao, then minister in Rajaji Cabinet, a classmate of my grand father. He and his friends were all unpopular for opposing Tanguturi Prakasam who demanded probity in public life. Venkata Rao was opposed by the rebel Nadimpalli Ramabhadra Raju. Raju's father Subba Raju only brought up and educated Venkata Rao. That added poignancy to the whole matter. Achhibabu is a major supporter of Raju. In all the villages of the island. But in Polavaram, I carried the Congress flag and was doing canvassing because Venkata Rao was a classmate and friend of my grand father. Achhibabu sent for me and asked why I am behaving like this. I talked of Gandhi and Nehru. He simply told they were not the issues, the bad behaviour and selfishness of the local leaders, is. I asked for details. He told. There were nearly 20 people near his Banyan tree. Then he caught my two ears and lifted and asked – what about Now? I ran home and asked my father, grand father and uncle. They all said the same. I ran back to his house. Still the congregation is on. I shouted Praja Party ki Jai! I was just 10 years old!

I ever remained an admirer
of Tanguturi Prakasam,
the greatest of all sons of Andhra
and a darling of the Kshatriyas, the Rajus.

In the canals and tanks, some one hurts or injures me – but complains to my father, he used to beat me without any enquiry. No wrong was done by me – yet punished twice! This used to be so all my life!

KARMA YOGAM AND PURUSHOTTAMA PRAPTI YOGAM

Later Routhu Sitaramayya took me to Muramalla on his cycle to show me Prakasam, in a meeting by him below the Banyan tree on Godavari Banks. I was kept on his shoulders. Prakasam hailed me from his chair. I went to him. He kissed me. Unforgettable.

During our tenure at Polavaram, I always returned home by sunset, the only fiat of my mother I obeyed without fail. After taking bath, my mother and me used to sit in front of the statue of Krishna that was given by her father a decade ago. I was made to recite several poems from different shatakams. The most important, however, was Bhagavatgita. I am to read Karmayogam –in Telugu script. And she will explain the meaning. After this I am to read the Slokams of Purushottama Prapti Yogam. According to her, these two are the most important sections of Geeta that a house holder must follow. Why? One must continue to do, whatever one has to. It may or may not bring success, but one shall continue to do. Secondly one must always try to become better all the time.

Even today
I continue to believe
in the greatness
of these two concepts
which I try to follow.

ROUTHU SITARAMAYYA - THE MAN OF THE VILLAGE - AND YANAM

I have never seen again a man so good and so useful to all people of the village. Whenever possible, I used to be on his shoulders holding his big turban or his cycle's rod!

There was a hilarious incident associated with him. In one of his frequent errands to Yanam, just 5 km and a ferry to cover, he was returning to Vedurlanka. He was on boat. Suddenly the boat was agog with alarm bells. All were astonished as to its origins. Suddenly the French police appeared on their petrol boat and found the sounds are emanating from Routu's body. The huge alarm came from a small time piece hidden in his turban, an attire worn officially by his cadre. Yanam was still under French rule. French goods were popular and often found, smuggled into the island of 8 villages.

Here mention must be made of island criminals who often escape to French Yanam. We once saw a gigantic man in chains, being brought to the detention centre in Polavaram. It seems he stabbed a man and looted Rs. 150 in the neighbouring Banapuram. During his escape to Yanam, he was caught in the middle of the river while crossing the ferry. He was a spectacle to the onlookers.

CHAPTER - 3

SCHOOLING

Polavaram

Duvvuri Veerabhadram

Education is the god that is experienced

Some great teachers – Madhumurty, Pentayya and a Guruji

Razole

Murders for promissory notes

Election Tricks

Cinema, Favourite Foods

Bhogi and friends

Jaggannapeta

Burma Palace

Hanumakonda visit

Learner's Feel

Cinema

Manepalli

An undeserving slap changes life

Classmates - Ramayanam

Ayyagari Master

Bhamidipati Parvateesam, the head master

Traversing floods for a competition

Stranded in an Island

POLAVARAM [Island]

As is the custom, around the age of 5, I was admitted in the school with fanfare. All children were called to the house along with the teachers. I am with new clothes and made presentable. Otherwise an unkempt and untidy street urchin. Teachers were given new clothes. Children were given some sweets and savouries – many were distributed by me. Some traditional songs were rendered. Every one thought my way-ward ways are reformed seeing so many boys and my mingling with them. Alas! This was only a passing hope.

For making me learn alphabets, so many people had to struggle and so many more had to spend sleepless nights worrying the future of a Brahmin boy. I used to be that much antagonistic to education. These efforts covered Schools, Tuition Masters and relatives in both Kesanakurru and Polavaram. No success. My earlier ways continued. Tanks, Canals, Fields, Groves –roaming everywhere playing all types of games mostly with non-brahmins as they too avoid education.

I was officially in the Standard-1. Occasionally, the school teachers used to send able-bodied students to fetch me from my house. I used to escape mostly. Sometimes caught, they would carry me bodily by a gymnastic method. They also announce loudly in a sing-song manner while carrying to every one's amusement. However, I was gathering some mass though rolling between two villages. This promoted me to 2nd standard. This was chiefly due to my mother.

MOTHER, A GREAT INFLUENCE

I am my mother's son. She always beseeched me to be distant from evil people. Because we cannot suffer, endure, resist, confront or fight evils. Only God can. But to react somehow is human nature. Yet we should keep clear. Yet they seek and chase you. You need strength to do your work despite them. I did this all my life. She built this self help syndrome until I left the School. How? Daily in the evening there will be prayers and recitations. Praying Krishna – an incarnation of God suitable for Kaliyuga. The recitations include Bhagavat Gita's Purushottama Prapti Yogam and Satakams – Krishna, Sumati, Vemana, and Bhartruhari. The impact of this evening prayers was telling during all my life. In the school, though I rarely went, I was good in all these to the Teacher's delight. Another was my liking for Newspapers gotten from my maternal Grand father, who used to hold daily conclaves on the current issues. Morality on one side and knowledge on another, a passport for grief and failure, were infused in me from that time! But in those days, they gave a promotion to next class and a wide spread affection.

DUVVURI VEERABHADRAM

One day, around noon time, I was playing marbles around the village deity, Pochalamma's temple. One tall man was standing and watching. I did not notice. As I suddenly looked at him, I got frightened. But he gave a broad smile, called me towards him and asked "you like this game". "Yes" was the reply. Come with me now. You resume after an hour – tell this to your friends. I obeyed. Speaking sweet nothings, holding my little finger, he marched through the street. Until a good building, where in the veranda were some dozens of children of my age group. He asked me to sit along with them. He gave a Clip-Board and pen. Another person dictated to the entire gathering some questions and asked to answer. We all were given Peppermints. Then he came to me and asked to go home first and eat food, then go to play!

This man was Duvvuri Veerabhadram, an uncle of our former Governor of Reserve Bank, Subba Rao. He was a teacher in the school and is a family friend. In villages all are family friends!

I returned home after dusk. My father was yet to return from his work. The two families are discussing how to reveal the day's developments, about which none knew except Veerabhadram! He first brought the news that I stood first in the entrance test and admitted to 6th Standard, 1st form – all with in a span of a few hours. My father daily used to enquire as soon as he returned from work, as to the mischief I made that day and start punishing. This day was more serious because of the countenances around. He had a shock of life- a pleasant one - and I was never punished again. My mother developed great confidence both in the advices of her father and my inherent nature. This identity of heart and mind among my parents, my teachers, my grand fathers and me has never faltered.

How I was admitted to 1st form was one story. But how a middle School suddenly appeared is a greater story that marched from New Delhi. Those were the times.

FROM DELHI TO POLAVARAM, THE MIDDLE SCHOOL

National Greats and The Local Greats: It was 1950, some base policies were being laid for the country. Patel was interested to strengthen the bonds of politics and administration. After all, policies need to percolate to people. Azad was keen on spreading the education to all levels. Nehru's focus was socialism; promote the economic equalities by reducing inequalities. All aims were good. And leaders were great, but un-achievable. Nehru announced that very soon land reforms will be implemented and the surplus land will be distributed to the landless and the tillers. This led to a national commotion. Heated discussions were going on as to the limits of the holdings on one hand, and registrations of lands of the landlords of all hues, in others' names - real and fictitious. Suddenly there was an announcement from Patel. Land reforms will be put off due to other pressing problems. Upper limit will be decided after a consensus from all Parties. But one decision is made and announced. Lands given in charity to trusts, temples, public causes, education etc will be exempt.

Lo and Behold. Within a short period, all over India, New schools came up; Schools became Middle Schools; middle schools became High Schools and high schools turned into colleges gradually. While the land is given by the local Zamindar, all others gave unprecedented co-operation.

What happened to such donations and how money bags indirectly took them back, is another story.

At Polavaram, Raja Kakarlapudi Achhyuta Rama Raju, affectionately called Achhibabu, gave the land in front of his Bungalow. Villagers gave Casuarina poles, Palm leaves for thatching and mat making, Coir ropes and what not. Women folk did their duties. Labour force erect the thatched huts with mats. House holders gave a variety of tables and chairs. In less than a month it was inaugurated by Kala Venkata Rao, a local friend, but a minister in Rajaji cabinet. He left for Madras, permission was sent by a courier and teachers were posted, both almost immediately. In a month everything was in place.

SIMILAR THINGS HAPPENED ALL OVER INDIA

In Madras Presidency, the Zamindars thanked Venkata Rao for saving their lands, middle and lower classes thanked him for bringing education to them, Patel and Purushottam Das Tandon liked him for a great compromise for doing what Sir CP Ramaswamy Iyer did in Kerala. But Nehru was upset and removed both Tandon and Venkata Rao from Congress leadership, President and Secretary, respectively!

If this middle school did not come, education would have stopped in many families. A few would have migrated, as there is no higher school facility for this island of 8 villages, then. The nearest middle school was about

3 and 5 miles after crossing either Gautami river at French Yanam or Vrudha Gautami at Annampalli. No one risked sending children 5-10 miles and crossing a river front! Even now, 65 years after this event the Kakarlapudi family is revered in all the villages, including me this far away.

EDUCATION IS THE GOD THAT IS EXPERIENCED

When I was in 3rd form [8th standard] my father requested for a transfer to a place where there is a high school for my further studies. Without waiting until the end of the Session, he was transferred to Manepalli, prematurely in September. While doing this, he was again transferred to Razole. Thus, I completed 6 months of 3rd form in one village and 4th form in a town. My experiences at Manepalli will be narrated in the next stage because I came back here for 5th and 6th forms.

SOME GREAT TEACHERS - Madhu Murty, Pentayya and a Guruji

There was a teacher, Madhu Murty Mastaru teaching Telugu. Of average built, brown coloured soft spoken and sweet. His pronounciation of Telugu was very good. When he recites poetry his distinction surfaces and adds to his sartorial culture of white dhoti and shirt. No one mistakes him for a Balija in caste. I missed him very much although I got another like him at Rajole.

Pentayya Mastaru was a kindred soul, lean, tall and black with slightly protruded truth. He rarely used to laugh but always conversing with students with concern and interest. He walks from Kothalanka with a few students, crosses Godavari at Kesanakurru where a few more students join him and continues the journey until the school at Polavaram. He always used to enquire the welfare of every student who meets him and all harijan students in the school. He was respected by the boatmen, all the harijan students and very few like me, I develop sympathies to him and his lads.

Guruji: I forgot the name of this great teacher – very shameful of me. He was many things to many people. He was staying in a small room in the house of the village Karnam. He was very good in drawing. Some of us would go to him for this. He was the drill master training us individual and collective exercises, calisthenics. He was good in Yoga teaching some of us Asanas. Photograhy was also his hobby. A great asset to all students and the local community.

We are learning the Asanas. My father was transferred. What a loss. This guruji used to control breathing and lighten the body. He used to lie flat floating in the tank waters, in Savasana or Padmasana, a wonder to on lookers. Such men are rare but were there in Munganda and some other places!

UNFORGETTABLE FRIENDS

Akondi boys always come first in friendship, but watched and guided by elders. Then come Annapantula, Mangipudi brothers – Venkat Rao and Subba Rao,

Nissankula Raja Rao. But Nambu Venkayya was closest to me. Probably I am the only one outside Akondi family who is allowed to play with Achhibabu's children, Cricket. We were openly playing Marbles, Tops, Hide & Seek, Carrom, Cricket, water sports in tanks, canals with or without cattle and many more not translatable into English. Even playing Dramas, is one of them !

RAZOLE

Razole is the Taluka capital of the southern most island, Nagaram. We just stayed here only for one year studying 4th form, yet is memorable for many reasons. This island has Vasishtha river as a border to the West Godavari District and Vainateyam tributary on which an aqueduct was constructed during British times facilitating water flow through a canal and peoples' movement on the road towards Razole.

I got a chance to experience several things all anew. I saw first a full fledged river, a steam launch between Razole and Narsapuram by river; another steam launch through a canal from Rajahmundry to Antarvedi. I also saw a Horse Cart. Cinema and Hotel going also began here with money stolen from my father's pocket. The school belongs to government.

BELIEF DEFEATS KNOWLEDGE!

In this school, I met a remarkable boy, George Suvarna Raju who was in D Section of IV form, when I was in A-section. A tall dark lanky smiling man – we became friendly. We were the first in the respective sections, and he was the first followed by me in the entire school. I left the school as my father is transferred. We again met in the college as classmates at Amalapuram, and renewed friendship. Upper caste students shun him as he is a Dalit. He was modest, mannerly, and cultured, which drew me to him. He was again among the toppers in Pre-University Course and left to join Medicine. Wherever he maybe, he will be an asset to society. We never met again. He must have been tutored by an exemplary Pastor or his family must have been influenced by Communism – the region from where he hails was known for both.

I first saw a great teacher, Venkata Ramayya, teaching Social Studies. We added "Jagruti" to his name because of his resemblance to the teacher hero of the latest Hindi film "Jagruti". His treatment of students is unparalled. From him I learnt of Buddha, as Bodhisatva and Jataka tales. His style of narration was spell binding. He is immaculately dressed in white with clean habits. Many of us used to assemble in his house in the evenings. Through his goading I learnt reciting poetry, musically. I got a prize also for poetry singing. He gave me a book "Udayasri" by Jandhyala Papayya Sastry as a gift which I kept for decades until it was destroyed by my own brother, a heartless chap. I could never find the teacher, not even his name. This trouble my conscience even now. It is to him that I owe some of my habits and strengths.

I also visited the Cremation Ground on the banks of Godavari, along with my mother as dictated by the local Tantric to propitiate the evil gods, during mid night.

Then only I realised that evils need to be propitiated, or stayed away and can be tackled only by antidotal persons, by looking evil. It was believed then that such inexplainable acts were necessary to cure my father's illness!

MURDERS FOR PROMISSORY NOTES

My grand father showed me the local Jail, Local Court, Police Station and a few criminals standing in the Witness Box. It was a sad and terrible Murder Case. We children went to the house where the murder was committed. When they were arrested and put on trial, we went to see how they look. Nine of them, killed a girl and her parents, broke the Steel Safe and took away the money and documents. The documents were the Promisary Notes by the debtors and original land documents. Fleecing the peasantry was an age-old habit in India. The sufferers had no other option than killing the Shylocks! This was in 1954! For a long time Razole had the record for the largest murders in India at taluka level. Fazilka was the second, and Kadapa was the third. These often exchanged places!

The whole town was agog with the news of 3 murders of a family of a Vaisya community. I was in 4th form in the high school. Many of us went to the canal side house where this crime was committed. So many stories went in circulation for some time. The culprits were arrested and the case came for hearing in the court. Due to my pestering, my grand father took me to the court. I saw the 9 accused. Standing on side gossiping merrily among themselves. They told the magistrate, that they had to kill the money lender not for money or jewellery but the promissory notes. For durations 5-15 years these notes continued with him; crops taken by him; yet the loans never ended; slavery continued leaving no alternative than to forcibly steal the documents with which he was threatening us of taking the land itself. Later I was told that many murders were committed due to this usury of money lenders.

My grand father also introduced me to his friend Kondepudi Subba Rao, his colleague in Congress now an advocate working for the victims and therefore popular with communists.

ELECTION TRICKS

When I am in the final months of the 4th form, elections came. As my grand father was a Congress man we went for electioneering. In one place, we saw a large enclosure, open-air with gates locked. Inside were a large number of semi-clad dark skinned people. Peculiar smells were coming. We were not allowed to remain and observe for long. On enquiry from the cyclists carrying the boys, we learnt that they are labourers in the rice and cocoanut fields, working under several landlords. They were given a few Goats, Liquor made in the sugarcane fields and a cook. They were to drink and eat and sleep off. This was meant to stop them from voting. Late in the afternoon, on our return, we went to the river side. We never found so many boats in the ferry. We asked the Yogi under the Bodhi tree, singing Kalagnanam of Veera Brahmendra Swami, what is the reason for this. He said that they were brought after the midnight of yesterday. They will go back today evening. This action was meant to stop the islanders from coming to the mainland, to vote. The landlords did not want them to vote.

Despite all varieties of such mechanisms, communists won on both sides of Vasishtha and the trend continued for many decades. The arch villain could not win even during the Indira Gandhi Wave! We went to the other side of the river and saw places where communists were tied to the trees and shot dead. Local people were excited that some knicker-clad urchins are showing interest in the problems of peasants and their exploiters. The shootings were done by the Malabar Special Police, based on the directions of the local Congress Chieftains. These instances were remembered for long, by many people.

VADREVU FAMILY, PARTHASARADHY, THE GRANDSON

My father was transferred to Razole area and I joined the local High School in the 4th Form. We rented a house suitable for our means. Opposite to our house, there is the house of a famous lawyer, Vadrevu Papayya. His family consists of 2 daughters and 2 sons, the youngest is our senior. This family is one of the most illustrious in the town. When we return from the school Papayya and his wife would be sitting on the parapet of their house; stop us for a while, me and Somasekaram, my class mate and ask us myriad questions about the school, class, teachers and what not. This would consume about 15 minutes. Then comes our other classmate who does not join us. He goes in and shouts for grand mother; then for grand father. He is Parthasarathy, the grandson of Papayya through the eldest daughter. He is very handsome and of upper class than me who does not yet wear footwear! I always stood first in the class that attracts other students, not his foot wear! I am prone to headaches, the migraine, undiagnosed by that time. One day I vomited while talking to Papayya garu. Then came out his second daughter, a Doctor from Visakhapatnam; took me inside, to sofa and to her arms and examining me. All of a sudden came Parthasarathy, gesticulated in some ways, went inside and shouted for his aunt, the lady doctor. On another occasion he pulled out a beautiful painting from my hands which was given by his grand mother to see. Then came his mother; chided him and told "See, you have to be nice to others; you are very handsome, tall, wear shoes, you have a cycle and we have a car - why angry with others? You share these with them, Sharma is first in your class, but always sickly, he deserves our sympathy and support like Somu gives, you also do the same. See his answer papers; learn how he got more marks; His behaviour changed for good, ever after, greatly.

BHOGI MISCHIEFS

The first day of Sankranti is Bhogi. We used to collect all waste or old materials and make a bonfire of them in central places and openly inviting others to join in the fun. The previous night some of us would move in groups to collect any such material. We also indulged in some other mischiefs. We used to change name plates from their places. Thus, a lawyer's used to go to a barber shop. Another lawyer's goes to a medical shop. Medical shop's will be thrown into the canal. Some wooden name plates will be consigned to bhogi flames. Sometimes we are caught and left with a warning and a smile!

Some friends were fond of sitting on trees for long and gossip. To continue this we used to collect oranges from the islands, cut into two pieces, chew slowly while gossiping on the Mango trees! Sometimes I used to move alone in the bazaar, to buy mixture and take home. From the same shop I am always tempted to eat Gulab jam on the sly. These two are the best I have taken so far. No parallel. After indulging in some of these I used to slip off from the merry makers to see a movie with a ticket to the floor! For these, I had to steal some money from home.

JAGGANNAPETA

My father was transferred to this village, about 3 miles from Razole. It has a Weaver's Co-operative Society that became sick due to member's corruption. It has to be turned healthy. There was not a single Brahmin in village. There is no house to rent us. Society is non-vegetarian entirely. And no High School to complete our woes. My family endured many hardships adjusting to them all. We stayed here for over 3 years in the society's building itself. Since I had a habit of moving in non-brahmin circle of friends, I had no difficulty. There is a cinema hall, good hotel, a canal and a ground to play Badminton, and a house for Carrom. I learnt cycling, swimming, carrom and badminton. Seeing cinemas continued from Razole. My father admitted me to Manepalli High School, instead of continuing at Razole. Both were equidistant from Jaggannapeta. A bunch of children from here daily move by foot to Manepalli and another to Razole, for studies in the high schools.

BURMA PALACE

A strange building exists in the main road of Jaggannapeta. Red in colour, it is a stately building double storied, something like the Writers' Building of Kolkata. It was constructed during post-war period, from Burmese Teak, excellent Masonry and Carpentry, planned and constructed by a returnee from Burma – Dommeti Balija Naidu to accommodate his entire clan. The architecture is palatial; the owner is definitely an unusually great soul, unthinkable to exist in those times and place. There are far more questions and doubts than the wonders the imposing large Burma Palace, generates. I have never seen him, but his grand son was my friend in sports and games.

IYER HOTEL, BETEL QUID AND OTHERS

The best thing in this town is the Idli immersed in Sambar in a concave plate in the hotel owned by a Tamilian, popularly known as Iyer Hotel. The taste of it is peerless. Matching to it is the sweet pawn we used to get from the small shop outside it. Nowhere I enjoyed a quid of this taste and flavour except the one prepared my wife, when she was young.

Another aspect of my life is many good things as well as the most bad thing were connected to this big village. It is here I learnt swimming, cycling, carrom and badminton. It is the politicians of this village posed friendly with my father but killed him by inducing a brain stroke through torture. In this place also, as usual I was addicted to cinema.

A Konaseema man was in the first Lok Sabha, representing Kakinada seat. He was a communist and hailed from North of Razole, Ramarajulanka. He was Kaneti Mohana Rao. He was forgotten during Golden Jubilee Celebrations, but for the initiative taken by Vundavalli Arunkumar, the local MP.

Petroleum Oil and Gas were emanating from some points in between Jaggannapeta and Tatipaka on way to our school at Manepalli in the premises of a Rice Mill, in the form of flames. It was a wonder for us children. After a few decades the whole region became a petro industry. A communist area supports a capitalistic cause. What a Paradox!

THE UNIQUENESS

This is a village dominated by weavers. Almost all houses have inbuilt weaving systems. All people take part in the profession; atleast in procurement and marketing purposes. There are several such villages in Konaseema. Bandarlanka, Pulletikurru, Mori, etc. In the yore, fabrics with very fine yarn used to be produced here, such as 120, 150 number quality. Such fabrics were used to be transported by Bendamoorlanka port. Clothes of such finesse are believed to be worn only by the angels, Devas of Heavens. Therefore the community got the name Devangas! While they are usually called Padmasalis.

HANUMAKONDA VISIT

My cousin brother was getting married at Hanumakonda in Warangal district. His family took me also for the function, I was then in 10th form studying at Manepalli, but living in Jaggannapeta. There were a few boys of my age group in the marriage party. So as to engage us we were taken to a nearby place, a great historical. This was the ruling place of Kakateeya dynasty, noted by Rudramadevi and her grandson Pratapa Rudra, Potana of Bammera, the great Telugu Poet and author of Mahabhagavatham, also happens to be from the same region.

We were shown by our elders and a local guide many things. This being our first exposure we were greatly excited. The big walls, the moats, the heavy doors, the arches were very stunning to our young minds. We were shown the village Bammera, where Potanna was supposed to have lived, many civil structures, and their utilities in their times. We also saw the temple of Rama where Potanna worshipped in those times. Later in the evening, we saw the temple with its thousand pillars. History was full of not only tragedies and victories but also wonders. I got initiation into something that I never came across before, and never left them after.

MANEPALLI

Another innings: I am in the 5th form. Daily starting from home with a carrier of food and books, walking about 3 miles either on road or by a short cut across fields to reach the school and returning in the evening by the same route along with the friends, five and half days a week became the routine. But these two years became so stamping on my personality that I realised fairly very late in life.

DEVADASI FAMILY

We enter Manepalli around school time. We were greeted by a melodious violin recital. We stop to hear. Sometimes some one comes to enquire what we are doing. We bluff – we want water to drink! A teenage girl comes and serves. We stare at her and continue. She is so beautiful and a violin wizard in the making. Later we learnt that they are a Devadasi Family of mother and daughter. One Saturday, on our return we saw a very elegant horse cart in front of their house. The horse was reputed to be from Kasi – so majestic. A tall, fair, lean and handsome man in Dhoti descended from it. The house lady came out to receive him with water to clean his feet, the beautiful teenager standing there with a towel to clean the feet.

The father is from Jayanti family of Pedapatnam, a few miles away. Wife was his second one from a Devadasi family; the daughter is his favourite child. She was a good singer and later became an exponent of Harikatha. A nephew of the father from that village loved her and married. He was employed in the Indian Embassy of Czechoslovakia. His wife died there during child birth and the husband left the job. What a poignant life! I did not know further about them!

UNDESERVING SLAP CHANGES LIFE

An incident changed my entire life and my perspectives on it. Incessant talking and laughing were among my bad habits. The teacher went out for a while. He came to the class to record student choices between Composite or General Mathematics. During his absence the class leader maintains order. Our leader was a Vaishnava Achari whom all of us respect. He had 3 vertical lines on forehead, half-shaven in the front and the rest of hair tied as a bun, a funny figure for us. He felt I was indifferent to him. He gave me punishment. I had to stand on the bench. As soon as the teacher came, he vehemently complained of my misbehaviour. He at once slapped me heavily, without an enquiry. He was our teacher for composite mathematics! I opted against the teacher. Not learning composite mathematics just to avoid an unreasonably punishing teacher. Thus, I closed many avenues in my career, affecting my own life! He was Nandyala Satyanarayana, an excellent teacher and a moral person!

CLASSMATES AND FRIENDS

I stayed in the school only for two years, for 5th and 6th forms. So many friends, some of these are from Jaggannapeta who accompany me to and from Manepalli

School. Some are classmates. Some from other sections. Some only for mischief making. And some from play grounds. Most friends were from Manepalli, Nagullanka, Pedapatnam and Manepalli Agraharam.

But the most memorable person was Ramayanam Surya Bhaskara Chatterjee. He used to come on a short cycle, from the West Godavari District after crossing the Doddipatla ferry. A live wire, available for any errand, a good Samaritan, a natural leader. His services to me were unforgettable. I often used to get Migraine Headache, which continues even today. Nausea, vomiting, weakness and vision problems are the other symptoms. I used to suffer almost for a day. Whenever I am attacked by these symptoms, Chatterjee used to command me to his cycle and rushes me to my house in Jaggannnapeta. This was the order of the Head Master. He would do this so happily. I never forgot him. But I never met him again.

A really close friend was Medicharla Subba Rao, my classmate from Jaggannapeta, a constant companion in most aspects. We used to come and go together to school by foot or by cycle. My friend in mischief was Rajyam and Ummanna. We three often escape from the school and roam about anywhere. We went to the canal side, river side, to Cocoanut groves for watching cock fights and betting. Once we crossed the river as there was hardly any water, played in island, flew kites, ate melons and returned. Then we saw the river in tide! Ummanna is Umamaheshwara Rao, the local Zamindar's grand son. Where ever he was sent for tuition, he would ask for my presence. That was our comaraderie. Our mischiefs were unending. Therefore, I was transferred to the next section, separating the trio. In my earlier section most boys were Brahmins, many from Pedapatnam. Girls also are here.

My routine changed in the next section. Most students were elderly. Brahmins are very few or nil. No girls. The first period was taken by the Head Master. The first duty was to tell the headlines of news to the class. This duty was mine. If I forgot anything, he would fill the gaps. I enjoyed this. Most students became my friends and admirers. From Nagullanka, families of Arumalli, Undavalli, Appana, Akula became friends of this tiny boy. The school leader would come to me for clarification of doubts. No Brahmin boy was approached by them due to absence of friendliness.

About the school. It was started by the Manepalli Zamindar, Bolla Subbarayudu, Ummanna's grand father. Some are full-fledged buildings and others, in the making. There was a separate playground. Sports and games were must for all. A variety of competitions used to be held. I used to get Prizes in annual competitions only in two – Jetitidharana, a Memory Test and in reciting poetry musically, the art I learnt at Razole.

The Head Master Bhamidipati Parvateesam, Teachers of Telugu, Social Studies and General Mathematics used to be very affectionate but stern with me. The tuition masters of Ummanna, Ayyagari Veerabhadram and Mangalampalli Gandhi also loved me. Those were the days! Ummanna was so good and I was so fond of him. He would not take tuitions unless I am there. Gradually Gandhi Mastaru improved his qualifications and became a College Lecturer.

Some friends at Manepalli : Subba Rao, Chatterjee, Jayanti and Prakasam, Akula and Appana. I had maxium number of friends at Manepalli and very good too. Jayanti and Prakasam were always mischievous. Medicherla Subba Rao was intimate. Ramasastry and Lakshmana Sharma, two dissimilar brothers were my friends, the former was very endearing. I have never and Mohan Rao forgotten him for taking me to their Citrus Orchard and entertaining. The drill master, I forgot his name, was also unforgettable. He made us practice High Jump, Kabaddi, Long Jump, Pole Vault, Kho Kho, Regimes, 3-legged Running. Gandhi Mastaru, Ayyagari Mastaru were unforgettable for their love and affection towards us.

AYYAGARI MASTER

Of these private teachers Ayyagari used to love students. He was a borne teacher. Smileful, I never saw him angry. An embodiment of patience and perseverance. He is also the village post master. He has a charming teenage daughter helping him and learning and teaching in the process. He was training the students in reciting, acting, singing, taking us for excursions to nearby places and what not. He was the most popular person among the children and their parents, among everybody.

Once in a drama of Harishchandra, I was given a small role as I was new to the genre. After several rehearsals, it was staged in the school on some special occasion. On the stage, I suddenly forgot the poems to recite, seeing the large audience! It passed on well otherwise. The master said no word but smiled. No one joked. I was happy to see one of his sons-in-law at the Cancer Research Institute at Adayar, Madras and recollect the days and times of this great man and teacher.

BHAMIDIPATI PARVATEESAM, THE HEAD MASTER

The head master was Bhamidipati Parvateesam, the youngest of three brothers – all famous as head masters. He was a class by himself. He is as kind as stern. He was respected by all teachers and the village elders and leaders. There are a few incidents that never went from my mind.

Because of our unending mischief, I was separated from Rajyam by shifting to B Section. He did not stop with this. He would take the first period. As soon as he enters the class, he asks me to rise and tell one by one today's major news – starting from international, then national and regional news. He then details one or two issues. This itself is a great training in itemizing, listing by some basis, after encouraging to recognize the importance of newspapers. The habits never went away from me.

INABILITY TO USE A CHANCE, TO ESCAPE

Complaints come to him. He calls the students and

enquires. He decides on the punishment. Mostly caning on palms. The caning is done on a platform in the presence of the whole school, in the very beginning of the next day. Me and Rajyam stand together to receive our due. First Rajyam extends his hand. As the master strikes on his palm, he withdraws his hand, a very deft move. A smart guy can escape like this using his cleverness – a concession allowed. My turn comes; I too try to withdraw the palm, but it is struck by the smarter headmaster. I take the full punishment and the leader escapes. All my life I took punishments for others. The headmaster many times commented "You do not initiate any bad activity. You cannot escape even when an opportunity is given". "How will he live his life." He lamented often.

TRAVERSING FLOODS FOR A COMPETITION

Once a circular came from the district headquarters inviting participants for an essay competition on United Nations Organisation at the district headquarters, Kakinada. This is open for students of 5th and 6th forms. It is being held on August 15th. The HM asked to take permission from parents and give the name next day. No one was willing. The HM asked me in the class, why not I go and get a prize for our school! I went home and got a written permission from my father. The HM gave a covering letter to Annadana Samajam and Anadha Saranalayam in the Cinema street of Kakinada. For a few days it was raining. Then floods began to rise. These two are a mere routine. With great affection and admiration the HM send me off. I was carrying a small Tin Box with clothes etc.

THE SAGA BEGINS

Chatterjee took me on his cycle to a point on Razole –Gannavaram Road. There I boarded a Horse-Cart and reached Gannavaram. A bus took me to Amalapuram and from there, another to Mukteswaram. Here I have to cross the Gautami ferry. There was a shock there. No ferry. Floods reached until the embankment. No crossing possible. That morning the authorities introduced a steam launch to ferry limited passengers. It just arrived. The conductor was unwilling to take a boy like me. Some elderly man enquired of me and my work. Learning all these, he became very affectionate, took me with him to the other bank on the launch and to the bus stand. He put me in the bus giving instructions to the Conductor of the Bus.

After a few hours the bus took me to Kakinada. As per instructions, I took a Rikshaw and reached the destination, Annathana Samajam on the cinema hall road. It is already dusk time. Starting around 9 am at Manepalli I reached Kakinada, alone, despite floods. It is getting dark. There is no where to go. Then came a tall and stately young woman in white, attracting attention and respect of every one there. On knowing about me, she came and asked whether I will stay in her house for the night. Happily I went with her, slept on a carpet, and moved to the venue of the Essay Contest next morning.

This lady was popularly known as "Ammayamma". She was the daughter of Justice Kanda Bhimasankaram and connected to several latter day celebrities. - Yechuri Sitaram, Palagummi Sainath, Kanda Mohan etc; She herself was a well known social worker of Gandhian mould.

The contest started. I began well. Very enthusiastic. Then comes the anticlimax. The pen stopped writing. There was no ink. I felt terribly ashamed of Myself I did not ask any one and I did not tell any one of this. I rose and returned the paper. No one intervened. I went to bus stand and from there to the ferry and returned by the same route, crest fallen. The shyness to express plagued me for long. Every one praised me for long, my boldness in taking initiatives. Many things in my life started with bangs, but ended with whimpers.

STRANDED IN AN ISLAND

Some students have a habit of skipping classes for an escapade. Me and my two friends Rajyam and Ummanna are no exceptions to this, although considered good students. After lunch we just casually walked to the river front. We found just a knee deep water in the river. We waded through them and reached the other bank. We continued wandering aimlessly. Somewhere watermelons are grown. We went. The caretaker gave us watermelon to eat and muskmelon also. Firstly, we are just children of 12-14 strayed lazily and secondly, Ummanna is the grand son of the local zamindar who built our High School. With the desk approaching and the place getting darker we ran towards the ferry to walk back to our houses. Lo and behold, the ferry is full of water and cannot be walked across. We started shouting but no one was responding. After some time Ummanna's people came searching for him on a boat and took us back to the other bank. Imagine a situation if he was not with us!. Only God has to send us a boat, with our parents worrying at our respective homes because no one would have doubted our escapade to the island! Courage comes often with numbers and makes one do unusual things.

MARCH-JUNE, 1957

So August passed. Quarterly exams are over. Half-yearly evaluations too completed. Every one was busy preparing for the all-important public examinations in March. Rajyam was standing first in Science, Telugu-1, English and Composite Mathematics. I was standing first in Social Studies, Telugu-2 and General Mathematics. I was second in English. Chatterjee is second in all papers. Tentative merit list gave Rajyam and Chatterjee to share the top positions and me the third. Month of June came. In Jaggannapeta I was playing Badminton, after which I went for errands with friends, untraceable to every one.

A teacher from Manepalli came on cycle to announce the results. The Telugu teacher from nearby Mogalikuduru first came to the only Brahmin's house in a Non- Brahmin village! Several people gathered at my house. As I entered I felt very enticing smell of some cookeries, all are smiling.

Then some one announced that I stood first in the school in the public exams with 20+ marks lead over others. Absolutely unexpected!

The school life of 6 years came to close. All friends of school of several years parted and went different ways. We come by an Institution and its training and spread far and wide and never to meet again. This parting pain comes back towards old age, grieving over golden times and hearts.

What next? The most educated man in our family, my cousin brother, Gopalam advocated me going immediately for Typing first and Short Hand later to get the necessary qualification before I am 18 years old. It will be easier to get a job and assist my father. This has been his refrain all along the years, or even decades. He was supported by all.

His younger brother, Mohan Rao came to my house. Together we went to West Godavari by crossing the ferry on Vasishtha, to Yelamanchili. My mother's eldest sister was living there. Her husband, our uncle was a school teacher. We went there to tell that we passed SSLC, 6th form. While returning after lunch, he casually asked what are our next plans. Mohan Rao said he is going to Hyderabd to join college. I said I will join typing classes at Rajole and later learn Short Hand so as to join a government job by the age of 18! He suddenly got enraged and asked why? Obvious reason, no money. He called his wife loudly from inside. Asked her to bring some box from some where. He took out Rs 500 from it and gave me to give to my father to admit me in S K B R College at Amalapuram. This was a shock for all for many years. He was never known to be generous. He told his wife, my aunt, he was the brightest boy among the 27 grand children of your father. It is our duty to help him in education.

A very interesting feature of my school days at Polavaram, Razole and Manepalli was the annual week when cultural activities take place; Winners of various competitions get open recognition with some rewards. During all the 6 years of schooling, I always received many prizes on the annual day which brought happiness and good reputation to my parents in the local society.

FIRST BOOKS READ

In this period I happened to read Veyipadagalu- the thousand snake hoods, at Munganda, depicting the story of Dharmarao and Ganachari apparently but actually the cultures existing then, their roots and significances – a magnum opus. But this was preceded by a compilation of history and culture of Andhra people called Andhra Sarwaswamu, in the house of Raja Kakarlapudi Buchikrishnam Raju of Island Polavaram. In the same village I saw the book Andhtra Rachayitalu by Madhunapantula Satyanarayana Sastry, while he was giving it to his grand father, Akondi Rama Murty garu, to whom it was dedicated. Udayasree was given to me as a present at Razole in some competition for reciting poetry. I also saw Sabdaratnakaram and Sringara Naishadham borrowed by Meru Subbanna Garu, but never returned. They belonged to my grand father, whose books were simply ransacked and stolen. Nobody bothered. I still have Geetanjali, the original edition. Bhagavat Geeta, Krishna, Sumati and Vemana Satakams were always in our house and even today, decades later.

ALLERGIES

I mentioned that I developed migraine. There were some factors promoting the dreaded headache. These are the allergies, the smells. First is the coconut oil smell. Another is the sandal wood smell. This led the whole family abandon these for my sake The third is petrol. In those times a horse cart was preferred to a travel by Bus. When it is inevitable, I used to request for a window seat. Sometimes this is not possible, I found that Amrutanjan and Lemon smell are antidotes for this allergy. Therefore the balm became my permanent companion ever after. The Manufacturing company needs to recognise and reward one!

CHAPTER - 4

COLLEGE DAYS

An Experimental Batch
Teachers, Students and Library
Field Trips: long, short and voluntary
Un-surmountable hassles?
Ajanta's Money Orders

NCC Addiction
Subedar Ajaib Singh's Advice
Progress card

The RSS, Blitz and Karanjia
Investigative Journalism
Values vanish, the Shop closes

Most important Pastime: Cinema
Avidi and my Father's Death
Non-recognition of Merit

ENTRY COURSE, AN EXPERIMENTAL BATCH

With the financial aid from my mother's eldest sister, I could join Pre-University Course with biology as the main subject. This course was introduced for the first time. We are the first batch, an experimental Branch. We had a full fledged English and Telugu, besides Biological and Physical Sciences. There was a tail of General Education. The environment was new. I am still in knickers, like many others. I was staying in a private room along with a cousin. This was of some help. After the studies, most of the time was spent in gossiping with friends- old and new - and cinemas, as there are no controls. After six months, I had to discard knickers, as I grew tall. I started wearing Paijamas in white as the cloth is the cheapest possible then. I started reading Blitz and became an addict to it. The year passed without any event. I just passed with 48%. I heaved a sigh of relief, for there was every chance to fail! Although I got a seat in B.Sc Agriculture at Bapatla, lack of funds prevented joining. I contented with a B.Sc in the SKBR College, with triple majors in Botany, Zoology and Chemistry. Most classmates were my colleagues in the previous course. A few failed in the last Intermediate but admitted in the 3-year Degree course introduced with our batch. Once again as an experimental Batch.

DEGREE COURSE, AN EXPERIMENTAL BATCH

In this programme, Languages were as heavy as the group subjects. While the group consists of 3 Majors –

Botany, Zoology and Chemistry, examined in the final 3rd year – the languages, Telugu and English, must be completed at the end of the 2nd year, along with a tail of a Humanities Paper. Studies were by and large neglected. Teachers are one reason. Youthful frailties and pranks away from families is the main reason. We had good teachers in Botany. The Humanities Lecturer was captivating. Zoology became interesting due to a new lecturer, Suryanarayana. There were some botanical trips, excursions to sea side and Andhra University, both conducted by teachers. Once we went on our own to Talupulamma Loya near Tuni.

For reducing costs, I intended to shift to B.A. and in fact shifted. I applied for permission and started sitting in these classes. But friends came in a group and dragged me out of arts classes and restored me back to B.Sc. May be all steps to reduce expertise may not be proper.

I was lucky to pass the languages just by the skin of my teeth. My attention was divided between studies and NCC. My financial problems were perennial. Some timely help used to come. One year I stayed at Munganda and used to daily travel between Amalapuram and Munganda. In the third year when all hopes vanished, two cousins of my mother - Vedavathi and Leela – helped us with sizable amount from the proceeds of sale of ancestral property.

TEACHERS, STUDENTS, LIBRARY

Teachers are appointed as per the rules of the University and preference of the College Managing

Committee. The teachers teach properly and disciplined. No tuitions. No extra friendships and socialising. Students are mostly from Konaseema. Girls are very few.

Library is not even a name sake. It just consists of a few wooden almirahs stacking books mostly donated by individuals. This made no impact on any one because hardly any one was interested in books, save some fools like me.

But it is here I read a lot of Sharat Chandra's translations, Viswanatha and several women writers of Andhra.

SESHA PRASNA

This is the title of a book, written by Sharat Chandra Chatterjee, in Bengalee. He wrote many and I was lucky to have read a few of them. Seshaprasna was my favourite. I read the translation. Sharat Babu raises many questions about women and womanhood, from several points of view. The unanswered question is : when a woman carries so many responsibilities from early childhood until death, neither she rebels nor the men feel ashamed at the imposed slavery, yet womanhood feigns happiness. This constitutes a complex question that plagues all thinking minds for decades. Sarat Babu argues tellingly and touchingly through the protagonist, Kamala. Is slavery, a kind of Contentment? This character has been one of my favourite characters in the world of fiction.

FIELD TRIPS: Long

When I was in college the teachers of Botany and Zoology arranged a long field trip to Vizag and Araku valley. We went via Kakinada specially to see Chaco's forest. Prof. Chaco, a botanist maintained a garden of a variety of plants in his own house. In those days it was a place for pilgrimage. His knowledge of plants and love of students were legendary, coming from Kerala state, for name sake!

Then we spent good time scouting on the shores – both rocky and sandy – for animal life. Then we were taken to the University to show the museum of the zoology department. Now only we felt we learnt the subject in the proper perspective. Next we moved to Araku – a totally alien experience. Climate changes. Food quality changes for better. Abundant Kamala oranges. Plantains are different and better. All things were purer. We roamed freely in the hilly forests coming across tiny tribal villages, tidy with dung surfaced houses and surroundings. There was excitement when Gnetum, an endangered plant was located by some one. Many trees we found there, were never seen by us before. What an excitement! The entire experience has changed the otlook of many people in many ways!

FIELD TRIPS: Short

Another field trip was much nearer and shorter. This time we took a bus to reach a place called Kandikuppa at the last reaches of Vrudhagautami. From here we traveled by boats to reach the light house. After 1-2 days of staying there, cooking and eating, etc all by ourselves, strolling the beaches, we started back, on foot because there was no water. This is due to a phenomenon called Ebb and

Tide. The tide variations begin far north, beyond Yanam, where the river Godavari splits and mingles with sea and salinity giving rise to Mangrove Forests. Two aspects need to be noted here. Morning time waters are in high tide and a boat is needed to traverse the islands – so small that they support only 2/3 huts, better called mounds. Secondly no point where the tributary Vrudhagoutami enters the sea can be seen. This raises the genuine question whether this is a mere lateral intrusion of Goutami from Vinjaram due to geological factors.

FIELD TRIPS: Voluntary

One activity in the college has attracted me. Otherwise I am a loner with NCC and Library activities. That is the group activities always organised by my friend Bhaskara Rao, a friend even now. Once we went to Kakinada on cycles just to see a cinema "Ten Commandments". We were about six on 4 cycles. After watching this 4-hour Saga, in a theater on the Cinema Street, we returned. I was unable to pedal. Bhaskara Rao carried me on his. We stopped at Draksharama; took bath in the temple tank, and sat for food that is supplied freely, every day. The server doubted the caste of Bhaskar Rao, as he is darker than others. Fortunately he was sitting next to me. I simply asked the serving Brahmin whether they have Komatis [Baniyas] in his village? He is one from our neighbourhood. He sighed a 'Yes' and moved on. Both skin colour, as well as casteism of untouchability were prevalent in those times.

Another outing was to Tuni, where Talupulamma Loya was famous for rich flora. We went first to Kakinada and visited Prof. Chacko's botanical garden, then to Annavaram Hills, thence to Tuni the last town of our district. It was like a hitch-hiking. We had no guide. Keeping on enquiring and moving on. This experience was indeed great – learning by oneself, managing ourselves, and returning safe. We were all below 18 years of age. And this is an example of the trust our parents reposed on all of us. And we are: Bhaskar, Bulli, Hanumanth, Subba, Viswanatham and myself.

SEEMINGLY UN-SURMOUNTABLE HASSLES?

First and foremost is the lack of money and means beyond school education. This means that I also will have a similar employment and salary like my father. But I will have three more brothers to be concerned with. They later were added by two sisters. Therefore, I have to raise my education and skill levels that might assure me greater incomes. Therefore, I must somehow complete a degree. A good work in NCC can help me in the job market.

Second, is my weak health. NCC can help or aid in my self improvement, vis-à-vis- health, both directly as well as indirectly.

Third, is how to excel in both to further my chances of better employment.

Fourth, is to safeguard my basic instincts and interests, while the time is spent for the above. This is to satisfy my soul, my conscience.

Of these the second and third are in my hands, the former by sheer hard work and the latter by intelligent labours. The last depends on the qualities of heart and mind and environment.

What about the first?

The all important money does not exist.

We cannot ask any one.

No one is likely to offer.

This issue was resolved by providence herself.

My uncle, luckily still alive, by chance came to our house and came to know of this dilemma. He gave all that he had- a mere Rs 500, a mighty sum at that time. My mother's elder sister's husband a communist doctor of repute just commanded me to stay in his home at Munganda, a village 8 miles away from the college.

When there was no money for the second year and the whole house is despondent and melancholic, two ladies visited our house to see my mother. They are her cousins - Leela and Vedavathi. – Our Lata Mangeshkar and Asha Bhonsle – In music. They came from Hyderabad to sell their ancestral land and carry back the cash. Knowing the condition, ill health of my father, lack of money, but goodness in studies. They gave Rs. 3000 to prosecute my studies, because education alone can lift the family. This is more than enough to complete the next two years. An unforgettable help.

Hoping against hope became
a part of my person from those times.

I completed 2nd and 3rd years of B.Sc by staying at Amalapuram, and brought satisfaction to my kind creditors and helpers. How did I fare – let us see.

The Second and the Third went on well. How? Ways of Destiny are mysterious. As far as NCC was concerned I attained all the best possible. In studies, I passed in 2nd Class that is creditable in those times, with the highest marks in Botany. These were unexpected by all including me.

NCC journey was a marathon and a saga of perseverance. In the first year, I was a butt of ridicule; was unable to wear and carry the uniform; trousers were not fitting; unable to lift the rifle. If the parade was slightly long and during the morning hours, I would swoon. Yet I never missed a single day in that year. I wanted to develop stamina. Further the two days of Parade gives me a good tiffin, free. I attended all Camps. Besides building stamina, camps provide free maintenance for a fortnight each time. During this time, I daily used to come on cycle from Munganda and return. A total of 16 Km. Along with me are about ten other students.

During this time my father was transferred from Jaggannapeta to Avidi in Kothapeta Taluka. The first year ended with full attendance in parades and camps, ostensibly due to interest actually due to economic and health reasons.

With this background, I landed in my new house in a new place, Avidi. It was summer. Two months had to be spent. Then a new routine emerged, all by chance, but useful.

The routine begins around 6 AM with a walk towards the canal which is a half a mile away. On my shoulder, there will be a towel. In my pocket, there will be an egg from the hen of our maid servant. On reaching the canal, walking along the canal banks, I complete, brushing the teeth with a local plant twig, defecate behind some bushes, and return towards the Cement platform and steps into the canal, meant for Avidi village. Before reaching the bathing Ghat the egg white and yellow are swallowed. Then jump into the waters after disrobing myself, swim for a while, and return home, around 8 AM.

In two hours, I complete at least 4 miles of walking, insignificant swimming, morning ablutions. But my worry of future was constant.

AJANTA'S MONEY ORDERS

My cousin Viswanatham used to send me Rs 10 every month by MO to help me in studies. Whenever the MO comes some students group around me. I had to answer their questions. One day he visited me also – a black man in white pant and shirt – both loose. When I introduced him to all those who gathered, it was an interesting bonhomie for a while. It is strange that there are so many brahmins quite well off. It never occurred to them to aid the needy students, which is done by all castes! He is none other than the well known poet Ajanta, the Deputy Editor in Andhra Prabha and a personal friend of the great poet Sri Sri.

The NCC ADDICTION

NCC gave me great satisfaction and also very good name. The story goes like this. National Cadet Corps was started in our college in the year 1957. The college itself began only in 1953. During 1957-58, I am not attracted to NCC. I was completely jolted during the Pre-University Course; in fact shocked. Of what? Of many things. Due to several problems, I have to face in the times to come, I thought of alleviations and preparations for future crises. It is to join NCC and work sincerely to attain a qualification that eases my future problems.

SUBEDAR AJAIB SINGH'S ADVICE

Ajaib Singh is our officer from the Army. He was disciplined and conscious of justice at the same time that I was more drawn to him than others. It is due to him that I took great interest in NCC and gradually nurtured an interest to become an Army officer directly through Services Selection Board. When I told him of this he just said NO. You are not fit, you will not be selected. But win a 'C' Certificate – use it to obtain selection in State Services as a Police Officer. For your low condition in finances but high caste condition, this is most suitable. If your problems are sorted out, opt for UPSC.

Years later, I found this to be the correct advice. I regretted and lamented for not following it.

NCC is also was fraught with problems that occur in society. Scions of privileged people wished to have their ways, leading to indiscipline which I had to curb as a leader.

Enmity ensues. John, Subba Rao and Narayanaswamy were my stead fast supporters because physically I was never a strong man! There are yet other friends – Suryanarayana, my cousin and Bhaskara Rao, my class mate who were my good friends in those days. Bhaskara Rao continued to be my friend until his death recently due to Covid-19.

PROGRESS CARD – NON-RECOGNITION

In the first year, I was a weakling pitied or laughed at. In the ensuing competitive examination, I stood first, due to enormous hard work for a few months which continued as a habit. I was given a Sargeant Rank. The same year I passed B certificate in B grade, the only one in the whole Battalion, the district. In the third Year, I became an Under Officer. I passed C certificate again in B grade, Battalion first. There were competitions for Quarter Guard Efficiency. I was the Commander of our College Team. We became victorious and brought a trophy. The first Trophy our college won thus was won through me. It is a great surprise to me and my friends that I was never even recognised for 2 district firsts and 1 interdistrict first and a Trophy. Great Mystery!

THE RSS

I am not a member of RSS. But all around me it was there. Their uniform and morning drill and their arguments, if you touch them. What is notable is their attitudes and behaviour. They were indoctrinated to help any one in need in the college and family, and they do and endear themselves. I experienced one man – Sripada Subramanyam – austere to the core like a Marxist, and a 2 years senior to me. Time passed. I had to go to Allahabad to attend the SSB interview. From there I went to Banares Hindu University, where Sripada was studying Masters in Mathematics. In two days, he showed me all Ganga Ghats, The small Big Temple of Viswanatha, and the site of the original deity, now a Masjid, with the remnants of the Temple. Another and more successful leader was the student Union Leader Varanasi Suryanarayana, the official chief of an RSS Shakha. He was my senior by 2 years and continued his work. His father was our Telugu lecturer. His son is today a National Leader, Ram Madhav. Most members are Brahmins. And an RSS member generally is a better person than one who is not.

BLITZ AND KARANJIA ADDICTION

A country bumpkin in school knickers enters the town to join the college. As he roams in wonder barefoot gazing at everything around, his eyes fell on a beautiful face on a News Magazine displayed by a shop. It was the then Miss India and the paper was Blitz which claimed to be Free, Frank, Fearless and First. My interest in the wide, wicked, world, then ignited continues even now. I was just one among a score in that remote island surrounded by sea and rivers. Karanjia tried to send Blitz to every town with a college. There were over ten thousand of them in those days.

Karanjia ran Blitz true to its meaning in German – thrust and surprise for an assured victory. Only it is different from its Hitlerite origins. I was hooked to Blitz. Catchy captions and exotic news provoked our innocent curiosity every week. While, most of the influences of Karanjia vanished from my mind, a few remained as his legacies probably because they are invaluable for a saner India.

NEHRU, SOCIALISM AND KRISHNA MENON

We learnt of socialism as different from feudalism and capitalism. V K Krishna Menon was inseparable from Blitz. Many of Nehru's advisors concerning Planning Commission, CSIR, UGC, ICAR, ICMR, Steel Plants, River Dams, etc are either Menon's friends, British or Indian, or their friends. In fact Nehru's affinity with the intellectual classes made him a darling of us and saw Menon as the catalyst. The role of Blitz in promoting their image was so great that some political forecasters like Hanzen considered a root-less Menon as a possible successor to Nehru in his book "After Nehru, Who?".

The Keynesian approach to economic development, chosen by Nehru was untiringly propagated by Karanjia.- Always a champion of egalitarian cosmopolitanism of the cities; in his case Bombay, and Menon became its embodiment who always won his election to parliament from here. He brought the entire cinema fraternity in defence of Menon and the city state. Ugly localism was created to defeat and drive him out ultimately. The filmdom itself was partly lost to localism which was in turn usurped by the underworld. The consequences of hatred towards Karanjia and Menon are here as the recent history threatens to be never-ending.

There was a heavy migration of Tamilians and some of them became under world dons such as Haji Masthan and Vartadaraja Mudaliar. Ramifications of these developments and fears they generated, ultimately invited back-lashes and emergence of Shivasena.

Karanjia went to the extent of lampooning Kripalani, a critic of Menon and received a reprimand from Parliament, a rarity, in our history! And what a scene he made in Delhi, before and after that.

PANCHSHEEL AND REVOLUTIONARIES

The menu here is ecstatic. Karanjia propagated the Nehru-Menon efforts in organising the newly liberated countries under the principles of Panchsheel. Blitz introduced to us other countries, peoples, cultures, struggles and leaderships. Sukarno, Nasser, Tito, Nkrumah, with Nehru became articulators of the aspirations of the newly independent nations, spoke-persons of the underdeveloped and then the leaders of the Non-Aligned countries, christened as the 'Third World'. Despite the Chinese, their efforts resulted in the Non-Aligned Movement – a fore-runner of today's South-South Co-operation and G-15. That these were brought to a common English-knowing public by Karanjia is no small matter! The heroism of Biju Patnaik came to light in this context, vis-à-vis Indonesia and Sukarno!

Also we were introduced to Spanish Civil War, Guevera, Castro and Granma, Ho Chi Minh, Yassir

Arafat, Martin Thong of the White Flag Revolutionaries of then Malaya, Mau Mau of Kenyatta and Patrice Lumumba of Congo. We literally wept when details of his torture and murder came to our knowledge! Head hunting tribes of Amazon were also introduced by Blitz!

ABBAS AND OTHER REGULARS

The last page of Blitz by Abbas is an education about India's literary and cultural ethos. That the Moplahs of Kerala and 'Bhayankarachari' of Kakinada and Rampa tribals of Andhra, were the only South Indian freedom fighters in the Kalapani, that Bhagat Singh and his comrades Rajguru and SukhDev were communists, that Muzaffar Ahmed was one of the founding fathers of Indian communism came to our knowledge here. Excellent features were carried here by Mistry, Raghavan, Jogarao and Talyarkhan. Also we learnt about Phizo and Reverend Scott in bringing about peace in Nagaland. Also about the efforts of Jayaprakash Narayan and his followers.

This was the only paper which brought to light many luminaries of India from Muslim cultures who richly contributed to India's great mosaic. Had this continued, there would have been a left extreme and a left of centre among the Muslims too, who religiously believe in brotherhood. Their marginalisation would have been stemmed. The plaguing vote banks would have never come into being. When the culture waned, the country lost its identity.

From a small rural town I learnt of India's greatness without any one briefing me. Abbas introduced to the readers many new things. It is here I learnt first about Premchand, Rahul Sanskrityayan, Mulk Raj Anand, Amrita Pritam, Pandit Sunderlal and Sahni Brothers. It is here I was introduced to Aligarh, which I visited later, Iqbal, Sahir Ludhianvi, Kaifi and Shaukat Azmi, IPTA, Kidwai, Jahir Brothers, Sadat Manto, Nazrul Islam, Humayun Kabir, Kosambi, Haldane, M N Roy, Omkarnath Thakur, Allauddin Khan. Novels like "Inquilab" and "Untouchable" were introduced to me here. And it is here that I came to know of a lame, a blind, a deaf and a stammerer adorned our first parliament – all communists, namely – Rama Murty, Sadhan Gupta, Bhupesh Gupta and E M S Nambudripad.

I also first came to know Hazi Mastan and Yousuf Patel, the fore-runners of India's under-world. Beverly Nichols and Catherine Mayo and Ugly American gave me a new perspective. Also Bhagat Singh, Aruna Asaf Ali, Achyut Patwardhan, Jayaprakash Narayan have entered my system. If the literary and political culture of Abbas and Karanjia was carried out, a strong left would have grown among the Muslims also with a telling impact. Consequently fanaticism, violence and terror would not have arisen or remained under internal checks.

PENCHANT FOR RHETORIC AND POLEMICS

Karanjia spewed invective on those he disliked. Coining phrases like proprietorials, Damn Fool Karaka, Kripalooni, CIA agent, etc, was his hobby. Piloo Modi, once provoked, entered parliament with a placard 'I am a CIA Agent' around his neck! Karanjia considered exaggeration as necessary for effect and Propaganda vital to blunt fascism! While most of his friends - Patriot, Search Light, National Herald, Link, Narayanan, Chalapati Rao and politicians like Rajani Patel, Aruna Asaf Ali, Ansar Harvani, Feroze Gandhi, Violet Alva, Bhagvat Jha Azad, Yashpal, Krishnakant, Dharia, Chandrasekhar, etc faded, his detractors flourished.

Not that everything Blitz did was good. I disliked highlighting the Shaw of Iran, rubbishing Ramnath Goenka, Proprietorials, Kripalani, Morarjee, etc. But the running battle with D F Karaka was very amusing. Alas he also has gone with his Current! Many shared his empathy but could not emulate because of his somersaults, difficult even to the Kalaripattu artists. An icon of youth, who built a non-communist leftist ethos in most parts of India through his resounding band wagon ceased to drum. When leftists wane, dark forces get unchained. All that Karanjia, Menon, Nehru and thousands of their admirers feared are materialising.

INVESTIGATIVE JOURNALISM

T T Krisnamachari, Mundhra and other affairs were scooped and figured in parliament. Feroze Gandhi became famous overnight. Investigative Journalism was given birth. Sainath, a winner of Magasasy Award and some other illustrious journalists worked here initially. This paper also killed an emerging Muslim Capitalist, Serajuddin, in his infancy, which probably, has deterred the emergence of entrepreneurship among Muslim communities partly resulting in their "backwardness".

COUNTER WEIGHTS

D F Karaka's Current, Patel's Mother India, and I S Johar's Column of Questions and Answers were a great attraction, and functioned as counter weights to the influence of Blitz on youth.

I always used to peruse Shankar's Weekly. Once there was an interesting cartoon. In order to lighten the burden on Nehru, the then prime minister, his ministers took away several ministries and responsibilities from him. The country was satisfied. Lo! and behold!, after sometime all the ministers were found to sit on the back of Nehru! This Cartoon by Shankar is one of the all-time bests.

In India, RK Narayan remarked in his "Batchelor of Hearts," bosom friends in Schools regroup in Colleges; they leave colleges to scatter in the wide wicked world, and never to meet! And I never went to Avidi Village. The soul of Peddi lies there with content. I did not go to other villages, where my soul and memories lie, and milking me mercilessly!

VALUES VANISH, THE SHOP CLOSES

Why such an historical tabloid, the largest circulated weekly of India for long, ceased to exist. This is a natural corollary to the demise of socialistic thinking, decline of values and deletion of revolution from our consciousness. With the destruction of Universities, where values are mostly nurtured, education died naturally taking the values with them. Only markets and products remain.

So the time passed away taking Karanjia, but leaving an ethos of India that valued all people.

Wherever youth are present some romantic or similar activities are inescapable. During our times a strange situation developed. Ramachandra Rao was a student of Commerce and a Sargent Major in NCC and very popular with all people. He fell in love with a girl from Tata Family. They are all known to us. Exams are approaching. And the fellow is unable to read without his girl friend. She too had exams. This became a big issue – temporarily resolved by allowing them togetherness for some time. There were stories of Kanakalata, a beautiful lady, but a widow after whom a rich guy was after. I do not know what were the consequences.

Devadasi related activities are a must in Konaseema, from times immemorial. I never missed these wherever occurred around Amalapuram at whatever scale. But never went nearer. What is attractive in these melas : youthful girls, beautiful people, dancing and singing – all in one place. Sometimes one gets a beauty with brains, or interest in literature. I have witnessed and enjoyed duels between Sukanya the most famous in those times, and some budding poets. She was of course became famous in later years, for her interest in literary and cultural activities, some famous writers of Andhra told me.

In a Mofussil college, an unusual but good event took place. Pratibha Kumari daughter of a Government Official joined the college. In short she was smart, charming, and vivacious. Every one wanted to have a glimpse of her every day and desired to talk, but could not. Some students started becoming smarter to impress her. This phase was good, and passed by.

The college had its share of turmoils. Agitations for one or the other reason or non-reason. Some times influenced by RSS, sometimes by SFI, sometimes spontaneously. Without these a student life is incomplete!

CINEMA, YET ANOTHER ADDICTION

It is not an exaggeration if we consider that there will not be any one who is not attracted to cinema, movies. I never knew what is cinema until I was in 8th standard, 3rd form.

In one of his trips to see his son's family, my grand father took me to Razole from Manepalli by walking about 5 miles. As I am a rabid questioner or inquirer, I was amused of a building, festoons, lots of people staring at wall posters. Asked of all these, my grand father told me it is a Cinema Hall, telling of stories from the beginning till end within 3 hours.

In the next show both were in the hall, Ravi Picture Palace – the cinema – my first one in Telugu "Pempudu Koduku". adopted or foster son. Most of the time was spent in weeping loudly attracting fellow audience. Ever since, I did not stop reacting to the scenes on the screen. Even on TV, I react. Sadness, anger, laughter are my usual reactions to the scenes shown.

At Manepalli, once my uncle came to see us. He took us on a horse cart, to a neighbouring village, Jaggannapeta, to show us a cinema. My parents and younger brothers. The cinema hall was Tulasi Talkies. Baiju Bawra was the cinema. No one knows the lingo. None of us understood. But we liked it for its music. We have an ear for melody. Language no matter.

For one year we were in Razole and for 2+years, in Jaggannapeta. All these years, I stole money from my father's pocket to enjoy a cinema. I went always to the Floor-Class. I never took another. And I never indulged in stealing except for witnessing cinemas.

Then came college at Amalapuram for 4 years, where there are 2 cinema halls. Firstly, I saw many Hindi films familiarised with their heroes and heroines and music. Even today, I am more enchanted by the smartness and beauty of Hindi People than our own. Equally the Hindi Music has captivated me more than our own.

One occasion to remember is the movie, Suvarna Sundari. I saw it three times. On the 100 day, some actors came to our town. The function was in our college. We saw Anjali Devi, Raja Sulochana etc. On another occasion, we saw 3 pictures one after another and cycled back to our village, some 8 miles away. Yet another incident was an adventure to see "Ten Commandments" in Kakinada town 25 miles away. Some six of us – classmates cycled this long distance to enjoy this celebrated movie and return next day.

I remember that we all decided that "Do Bigha Zamin" as "Dhobi ka Zamin". Such hilarious events were a myriad! But we empathied with the suffering, talented, unlucky and good people. Often we are enraged at the evil-doers. The cinema promoted sensitivity and goodness among most of us.

Really I moved from wetness to dryness! I took admission in Pilani, now, BITS, at the eastern edge of Thar. There was no cinema hall in Pilani and neighbourhood. But the institution screened every Saturday a film, mostly in Hindi, in an open quadrangle. Only 16 mm films are shown. This was our lot for all the 8 years I was there.

Are films only for entertainment? Nay. I can share my experiences. Others also will have some variants of this.

On one side, it is music. Besides the classical, we hear many folk forms that we never knew. On the other is lyrics. They are far more meaningful than the celebrated poetry. When translated into English, they outclass some celebrated poetry. Sahir Ludhianvi, Shailendra are fantastic, others not lagging behind. This constitute our composite culture of India. The stories constitute another aspect of India. We became familiar without labouring – the literature ! Not only Tagore, Sarat Chandra or Premchand but also many others from other states. We came to know Ananta Murty, Vasudevan Nair, Kushwant Singh, Amrita Pritam, to mention a few.

Thus, I am left enriched by Cinema in literature, music and poetry –and the state of our society. Do Bigha Zamin depicted the future that was in store for India, as a warning signal to Indians. However, scientific one may be or secular, we cannot escape "GOD" one time or the other – several films have shown. All movies tell us that womanhood is more a curse and has to be borne with forbearance.

I told that I was pilfering money from my father's pocket to see cinemas. I feel he knew this. But I was getting marks. Otherwise possessed good habits. Probably he judged that cinema gives psychological inputs leading to good performance in life. In fact Cinema is an important activity of all societies at all times. The medium is such.

Different people have different favourites. Heroes, heroines, in differrent languages. In our town we used to get Hindi films sometimes Tamil films. In both the cases there used to be an interpreter in the hall loudly telling the story. I used to like Dev Anand and Raj Kapoor. My favourite film in those times were Do Bigha Zamin depicting the rural migrations to urban systems in search of livelihoods. Another was Jagte Raho – the mischiefs in society if only we keep our eyes open. Other people have other preferences. And these shift from time to time. I used to see at least 2 cinemas each week. I used to go alone because I can freely go to the cheapest enclosure!

AVIDI AND MY FATHER'S DEATH

Vedaraju Satyanarayana was my colleague at college and a very good soul. He was my sole financier whenever needed always on a returnable basis. He kept this relationship confidential. All good things about me used to be told by him in my house and in his house and other friends. He told in the village that while all students studied for a degree and obtain a qualification to go to next stage, Sharma obtained another qualification too, to enter Indian Army directly as an officer the first student in the entire college until then.

Every evening, I would go to the canal side and walk to Kothapeta. There I pick up a ready person Chamarti Krishna Murty, my junior at Amalapuram. Together we walk to Mandapalli, pray at Shani temple, and return to his house, take a cup of tea before embarking on the remainder of journey to Avidi -a total of 10-12 kms of happy walking, a memorable exercise.

When my father died in 1964 December, our stock was good. I am the one doing a Ph.D. There was a Doctor, an Engineer, and Petro-Chemist – all were my friends. Their families respect us, come to my home whether I am in or at Pilani. The village respected us. There were even marriage proposals. We could have settled there, with friends, instead of going to a psudo friendly Munganda. They are the people who floated a vicious rumour that "The dead body of my father was not allowed to be lifted until the debts are paid" to show how uncaring I was ! It revealed prejudices never wane.

The great college life ended. Venu, always with a cycle but never seen riding, Brahmin-baiting Venkanna-Gangaraju- Bandaru Satti, Good Samaritan Bhaskar Rao, Vintage Rowdy Achari, Class Conscious Exclusives, Brahmin-conscious Karra and Sripada, Communist Kishtappa, Sex-obsessed Yerram Raju, Ramanatha Sarma, Noble Rajus, wise people like Vedaraju Konda, Vivacious Pratibhakumari – all will be missed. And new ones enter, in addition. But Humorous Venu and hilarious Bhamidipati Brothers are unforgettable and unreplaceable.

SOME PERSONAL EXPERIENCES

The most unforgettable experience was the accusation in the house we were staying that I have stolen some money from the room of a person named Venkanna in the final BA. It was a shock beyond my ability to bear. Many students condemned him for the accusation, for they know my character. Unfortunately for the Brahmin hater, the money was found misplaced by evening. He never repented for his hasty act. I never talked to him.

Another cruel act was by the HOD of chemistry, G V S Ramarao. In the final exams, I seem to have broken a beaker. I was to pay 56 Paise as fine. It seems the levy was notified in the notice board. I did not notice resulting in the non payment. The officiating principal i.e., GVSR sent this failure information to the university. Therefore, my result was withheld. For over a month. We could not know. A friend in Waltair went to the university office, found the fact and paid from there. The result was then declared. I obtained a 2nd class; the time to apply any where for higher studies lapsed.

After the exams are over we rush to homes. They could post information to homes. Or send message through some local students. I for one would have paid this huge sum of a fine. He and me saw each other several times, but did not tell me. I am not known to be a bad student in any respect. But he did this.

I had a habit of writing notes. No one was interested in it as I was not considered a good student due to my over concentration on NCC. However, I passed B.Sc that too in a 2nd class. My notes became wanted and popular. Then came two friends – cum - relatives – from Munganda, the Khandavilli Brothers who asked me for notes. I just gave them. I would have given to anybody who asked. They happened to be the first. The duo, the tall and the short, are complimentary to each other – two types of diplomacies at play, for a success at any cost. They did Masters in Botany and Zoology from BHU and BITS. respectively.

NON-RECOGNITION OF MERIT REPEATEDLY

I was very prominent in NCC. First as a Sargeant selected strictly on merit; then in practice as a strict, disciplinary and impartial leader on duty. I became further famous because I passed certificate B, in B grade - the only one in the college standing first in the whole Battalion. During this time I was selected to be the leader of the Quarter Guard by the Associated Staff from the Army. The team selected had 3 seniors to me. They rebelled against me in the camp where the competitions are to be held. They were given 2 options. They will be replaced. Or they have to wear lower rank insignia. They did the later. Thus, Sargeant Major, Under officers worked under my command. In the competition among some 15 colleges, we won the championship and the trophy, the first for our college. Next year, I passed the

Certificate C, as an Under Officer, and in B grade. Once again I stood first in the Battalion.

None of these were reported in the college Magazine and none recognised in the annual celebrations ! I never knew the reasons for this hurt to an achiever. Later some one guessed that the 4 officers, all Brahmins, were responsible for this sin. Why? I never gave them any importance. On the contrary the army personnel were preferred. This made many cadets do the same. Moreover I did not request them to get me this recognition !

In this connection let us ponder over this famous quotation!

> *The notice which you have been pleased to take of my labours, had it been early, had been kind; but it has been delayed till I am indifferent, and cannot enjoy it; till I am solitary, and cannot impart it; till I am known, and do not want it.*
>
> **Dr. Samuel Johnson**

FRUGAL LIVING

In the college, I used to prefer isolated living than in lodges or together with others. Main reason is my comparative poverty. I developed Spartan habits intentionally – living on floor, using Lifeboy soap, Protex Talcum powder, wearing pyjamas because pants are costly and wearing no foot wear. Group outings are avoided – to cinema, hotels, just merry marching. I scrupulously maintained a studied isolation during all my 4 year college life as a means of economy and hiding my humble means, lest I may be looked down. Because I was good in studies, my basic habits and intentions were camouflaged.

One of the merry makings in the college was eating competitions under betting, for fun. I used to participate and win too. Normally a 5-rupee note! Further I joined NCC for reducing my costs. They used to give Breakfast on 2 days. In all the camps, for a fortnight each, twice a year, rations are free. But I was duty conscious and disciplined due to which I won some laurels and good reputation. Under this cover, I could hide my original intentions.

HUNGER STRIKE

There was a strike by students and a procession. The cause was to reinstate a lecturer who was dismissed for want of mental balance. Hunger strike was one of the pressures. No one was willing to sit in fast! I sat winning a temporary glory. Fortunately the strike was called off by afternoon. And a dark, tall, man in white pyjamas came and gave me orange juice as a mark of breaking fast. He was Ganji Nageswara Rao, the local communist MLA.

ATTRACTIVE GIRLS

I was associated with girls right from the childhood. Firstly 3-4 neighbouring girls used to come to my mother to learn singing. They were all used to be fond of me, especially one of them, Kameswari, Akondi. As my handwriting used to be good I wrote for her Kirtanas of

Tyagaraja, Tarangams, Ashtapadis of Jayadeva as they learnt from my mother. These are remembered for decades in the village of Polavaram. At Manepalli I was, like many was fond of Ramalakshmi, my classmate for three years. At Razole it was Buchhaammanna, my classmate. During my entire 4-yr period no one was attractive to my eyes in the college. But outside, the youngest sister of my lady classmate, Suvarchala and the Garimella girl next door in Avidi village where my family was living, were very charming. These are mere teenage attractions of passing nature. Yet they tell our tastes and their longevity. All youth will have this as a common habit.

SOME UNIQUE WOMEN

I have come across or experienced great qualities with a few women, albeit different from each other. Subbamma, of Polavaram, Suramma of Razole, Manemma of Jaggannapeta, Peddi and Kameswari of Avidi, Ramanamma of Kesanakurrupalam, and Kavanna of Elamanchali. Subbamma was a Brahmin widow with a shaven head wearing the prescribed white dress. She had no children and no near relatives but was left with a house and some property. She lived with cats and dogs. Who ever gets a job at Polavaram, they stay in her house. She was an open street fighter for the cause of especially women. She prevented alone violence in the families. She did not allow the barbers to shave women' heads. The village Karnam's sister had to go to Kasi, to shave head and become a widow! Suramma, a carpenter's wife, was similarly a fighter for justice in the neighbourhood, very helpful to all the needy. Manemma is the wife of a Weaver-House holder. She was an advisor and quiet helper and satisfying the needs of otherwise helpless people. Peddi was an old domestic help from Kapu community to whom I was personally indebted. She used to give me an egg per day, and gave me all her life's savings of 460 rupees and asked me to go to Pilani for higher studies! Then there were three Brahmin women who suffered enormously due to male tyranny and authority. They bore everything with fortitude and succeeded to survive – Ramanamma, Kavanna and Kameswari. They are very fit to be the heroines of Ranganayakamma Novels! Two of tham are my relatives.

UNPREFERED AS A FUTURE SON-IN-LAW

Parents of daughters normally will be in the search for eligible grooms. Sometimes their eyes fell on good candidates but without adequate finances. One way to convert this situation to their favour is to offer financial help for the future studies of the good student. If accepted, this family virtually buys up the future son-in-law. They cover all the expenses of higher education. Before the education is completed marriage with their daughter will be solemnised. We were looking for an offer of this kind, as it happened with some friends. But nothing has come. It was both a shock as well as a surprise, because our family as well as myself had reputations. Later I understood it is due to 4 siblings considered as a great burden ! And a false rumor that a marriage contract following the above mechanism is already fixed, and on course!

MY LIKELY HELPERS

Everytime after SSLC I needed help to prosecute further studies. This came at right times entirely through providence. This continued until the Doctorate degree without me begging for it. If I had to approach, I would not have gone to any relatives or fellow Brahmins. I would have requested for help [1] Achhibabu of I. Polavaram, or [2] Bolla Zamindar of Manepalli, or [3] Kotireddly of Kadapa. I would not have approached any of the beneficiary families of my grand father when he was affluent – Narasimhadevara Satyanarayana of Alamuru, Bikkina Venkataratnam of Ramachandrapuram, and Mallipudi Pallamraju of Kakinada, a very famous family of Andhra.

Fig. 13: Group Photo of Students of Pre-University Course at S K B R College Amalapuram, 1957-58, where the author studied.

Fig. 14: Group Photo of Students of B.Sc at S K B R College Amalapuram, 1958-9, where the author studied.

Fig. 15: The Author as the Under Officer of the NCC [and a 'C' Certificate Winner, who won many laurels for the College.

CHAPTER - 5

UNIVERSITY LIFE IN PILANI

Survival, a Miracle
Regular features
Study tour to the hills
Death of my father and its aftermath

Culinary exercises
Surendra Babu, Rama Rao & Pranab Ray
Sanjeevdev and Janakiram
Foreigners

Loosing a lecturer post
Jayasree Tea gardens – money vs contentment
My Doctoral Thesis

Ethics in Science
Absence of Mentoring
Some queer incidents
Champions without Trophies

Mutton soup for me
Prof. Morris of Chinchinada University
Season for Cupid
My biggest regret
Jhunjhunu Court with Muley sab

My admission to Birla College, Pilani in 1961 was a turning point in my life, thanks to Prof. M. Suryanarayana [S V University, Tirupati, Anthropology], then my classmate who gave me the application form and forced me to fill and post. I left for my village. Within a week I was intimated of my selection. But the jubilation was short-lived. There was no money even for travel. This disappointment was noticed by our old maid servant, PEDDI [elder mother]. She just went back to her house and returned with a cotton sack enclosing a small earthen pot. She poured down its contents and asked me to take it and go. This cash, all in coins, her life's savings, was Rs 460 an elixir that led me towards Pilani and the rest of progress.

FIRST EXPERIENCES: SURVIVAL, A MIRACLE

This money saw me through until September, when I was asked to quit for not paying the mess bill. My friends from Physics, led by Surendra Babu, told the Warden that I had to leave studies for want of money, which was in turn informed to Botany Department. The faculty lamented to their wives by evening. Our Professor's wife summoned me to tell not to leave. She asked the warden, a Botany Lecturer to lodge me in his house, in the front room. The Professor kept the Bill payment in abeyance until further orders. A scholarship of Rs 15 was granted - the condition was that I have to study my best and be very regular. I stood first in the half-yearly exams and the stipend was raised to Rs 45. In the annual Exams, again I stood first. In the second year I was appointed a

Part-time tutor with a salary of Rs 100. During these two years, and for many more years I was treated like a family member by all my teachers and their friends in other departments. To me Indumati Muley, My Professor's wife became my second Mother, Mummyji. Her affections, attentions and concerns were even greater than my own mother!

I was exposed in my class to - Malayalees, Punjabis, Bengalis, Rajasthanis and Hindi people. Among my teachers – Marathis, Malayalees, Pahadis and Punjabi. By the year end I had known Biharis, Oriyas, Kannadigas, Tamils and Kashmiris – covering some 16 linguistic families! It was India. For a villager in an island and a student from a new Taluka College this was a revealation as well as revolution. What I became there were sharpened and stabilised by IISc where I worked as a Post-Doc later on. Foundations thus laid could never be shaken. Structures were felled! I rebuilt. They were felled again. I built once again. That was the BITS plus IISc plus Raw Island Villager's Spirit!

A major interlude - a profound and poignant period began in 1965 when I faced two tragedies – one after another and each had a sequel of accompanying social tragedies – which haunted and hounded me all life – threatening my foundations with severe consequences. But these helped me to keep my head high alone in any flood or fire from small minds.

REGULAR FEATURES

A regular feature is the annual visit of Shri G D Birla

and his family to meet the faculty and students. This is done on Basant Panchami. In the lawns between the Institute and the Sharada Mandir in front of it, all sections of the Institute assemble, around a tent that houses refreshments. The tents were organised on either side of the lawn, about some hundreds of meters in length. The entourage consisting of GD, other senior scions of the Birla family, Director, Deans, Registrar, Birla Education Trust, used to move in between the rows slowly stopping at every tent and making enquiries about their welfare and receiving suggestions and complaints. Research Scholars tent used to be the first on the right of the VIPs. I was selected as their leader and spokesperson, I was a Research student. A great privilege to receive and shake hands with the great Birla for three years!

Another constant feature are the visits of famous and accomplished people. They mingled with students after talking in the auditorium. I heard Morarjee Desai, Humayun Kabir, Swami Ranganathananda, Prof. V. V. John, ECG Sudarshan etc. The most inspiring lecture and discussions are by Swamiji mostly on Indian heritage. The most humorous speech was from Prof. John. His target used to be Americans. That was the time when the book "Ugly American" appeared. He regaled the audience during his several visits from Jaipur, talked mostly on human hypocrisies and social sins in impeccable English. Sudarshan was a young scientist dealing exclusively science and its historical contents and practices. We remained friends until around 1990!

The facilities for sports and games for all – both indoor and outdoor – and a gymnasium, are unparalleled! It is here I learnt Shuttle Badminton, Table Tennis, Billiards. All newspapers in English, many Magazines including Time, News Week and New Scientist come to the Club for Faculty and Research Scholars. There is also a Gliders' Club. I learnt many in door games. But not Bridge, a traditional favourite of many. I could not learn Tennis although our teacher Dr. Ambuja Pillai could . She was the wife of our second Professor, Prof. S K Pillai.

STUDY TOUR TO THE HILLS

During the Masters course, there will be two field trips – one each year. First year- I did not go. But in the second year, I went. This trip and the times preceding and following it were also very memorable. In short I gained the goodwill of my teachers as well as my classmates, thus a foothold in society at Pilani. The trip planned by teachers was to Dehradun, Mussorie and Nainital. Professor Muley accompanies, but without his wife, and for the first time. She gave her responsibilities to me! Assisting Muleysab in the carriage of ablutions in the morning, giving timely medicines and the like during meals times. I got good name not only from the professor but also the colleagues and latter his wife affectionately called by us, Mummyji. During the trip, classmates nick-named me, Mummyji!

The first stop was Delhi, where Satyaji joined our troupe. She was three years senior to us, a scion of the owners of the famous Narula Hotel in Connaught Place, working for a Doctorate under M.S. Swaminathan of Indian Agricultural Research Institute. She gave us a grand dinner at her hotel and later some of us including Professor, went to a Cinema, Anpad, in Moti Hall in Dariyaganj. I had to sit next to Muleysab as a caretaker. This responsibility continued.

We first stopped at Dehradun. We were taken to several neighbouring places for observing plant diversity; then to Botanical Survey of India; where we met Dr. N C Nair, a former student of our professor and a Lecturer at Pilani until a year ago. Our next visit was to Forest Research Institute. We met Dr. Venkatesh formerly of Delhi University, who took us around and explained so many things of forestry and Indian forests.

For a day we were taken to Haridwar. We stayed for a night in Birla House on Ganga. The back part of this house is regularly bathed by the Ganga waters. There were steps. Some of us took a bath in these very fast currents. Others went to Harki Podi. This was a great experience for me as a caretaker of Professor. We disrobed ourselves to a minimum and stepped nervously into a stream purposely deviated from the main Ganga. Of course, there were steps and iron-chains to help the devotees. Into this I led Muleysab. On the otherside was Trivedi. Around us were a few students. The whole mass went to the cold waters to take a few dips in waters. Shivering, we came out, un-wetted ourselves, re-dressed to move to our residence and thence to

Dehradun. Our vehicle was driven ahead north-wards to have a glimpse of Rishikesh.

We then moved to Mussorie. The notable point here is the skating club. We were taken to the Institute of Indian Administration. The director Dr. Ramadurai and Muley sab were friends in England, where they were students. We saw the future administrators of India, the steel frame of India. We sat with them, to hear the lectures meant for them and we dined with them. We saw the manners of the elite. But none of us were inspired to be motivated by their paths. I always regretted this. This is a failure of the intellectuals at Pilani who fell into the capitalist trap of early satisfaction in life and forget their intellectual responsibilities and to regret in leisure, very late.

I used to stand outside the bathroom when Muley sab takes bath awaiting his safe return.some other students used to keep company. One day a song was heard from the latest Hindi Movie. "Sow sal Pahle, Muzhe tumse pyar tha, aaj bhi hai" and so on. For some we were debating about the origin of these sounds. Lo and behold, Muley sab opened the door crooning with a smile! Eversince the song became popular in our department.

Next sojourn was Nainital. The same routine continued. We did not see any one but the Himalayas and Nandadevi peak. The lake offered a grand view, the type of which is not present anywhere in India. Boating in that is a routine pastime with lights all around the lake, Nandadevi at a great distance and finally the great lake. Imagine the impacts of these crowded days and nights on young minds!

BACK TO THE BASE

It did not come to my mind at all at this time that going to US to get a doctorate there would have earned me enough money to fend my family here. Unlike others, I did not take this route. I also did not try for Competitive Central Services as some believed that my good general knowledge and reasonable English would have made me successful. But I was enamored by a doctorate degree, a rarity in those days. I wished to be like my Professor, Babu Narhar Muley! Having failed in the Services Selection Board to directly enter the army as an officer, I was stuck to a doctorate, on the rebound, and never altered my vision. In later life, I found this tragically blind!

I joined research in September 1963 and was able to support my family with Rs 50 per month. The progress had been slow but steady. All appeared fine as never before to me and my family of parents and four siblings. The apple cart was upset, drastically. Life changed tracks ominously for me. My father died in December 1964, leaving five people to be tended solely by my scholarship, among other consequences. I had to weather pressures to discontinue research and seek a job in the neighbourhood. Due to my room-mate Ananda Rao's help in cooking, I managed to send Rs 150 to my home and live with 100 in Pilani. The tragedy and hardships for both me and my family did not end. My professor and benefactor passed away in December 1965. My great prop disappeared.

My father's death was a "murder" appearing natural. When he was recovering from a minor stroke a few people guilty of embezzling public funds, hostile to my father for reporting their crimes to higher authorities, entered his room and abused him filthily. They were jealous of my education They left but the stroke returned taking his life. They were never punished. God is still waiting. The death left 5 orphans under my fragile guardianship, preventing the fruits of education from maturing.

And my own guardian angel passed away. No. He too was "murdered" by the first Director of BITS. Laxminarayanan by publicly insulting him on some pretext. He, like many others was jealous of my Professor B N Muley for his popularity and reputation in the entire campus. We were shocked; all science departments were shocked, but only one had guts to protest in a subsequent meeting. He went home; fell sick. I was always the caretaker of his house and his dog Jimmy, but my guardian angel never returned. All members of faculty were threatened. As usual there was one Quisling, rest made a beeline and compromised by pleasing the Director. I never visited him. I became an orphan, later, a victim.

I became thus, from a guardian of five orphans, an orphan myself in the pursuit of a PhD and furtherance of research interests.

My attempt to obtain a job there in 1967 was thwarted by an heartless and vengeful Dr. M.C. Joshi, my teacher and now Reader and head of the department, deliberately. No faculty reacted, only some researchers. I did not show my resentment nor sadness, but remembered forever, for, it was the first injustice meted to me in my long life. And the train of injustices continued to run unstopped; only pausing occasionally for a refueling!

CHANGE OF TRACK

In college, I was in NCC and acquitted myself very creditably with a "C" certificate in "B" grade, and first in the Battalion. I naturally applied for a Commission in the army. I was called for an interview with the Services Selection Board at Allahabad. This was in September 1961. I was not selected in a 3-day selection process – only 2 made it out of 20. But at Pilani, I stood last in my class in the Quarterly Examination. Further I was selected from Rajasthan to participate in the Republic Day Parade, on 26th January 1962. Both these angered my professor but gave me a promise of scholarship as well as a warning. Therefore, I concentrated on studies and abandoned the Army dream. That I stood first in the Half-yearly and changed my road is another story. After the Chinese war in 1962, NCC was made compulsory but there are no trained personnel. I happened to be the only one in Pilani. So I had to wear the Uniform of the Under Officer and organise the Platoons and companies. Next to me is yet another Sharma from BA. We had a great time and fun in serving the cause of India.

It was a challenge. A certain prophecy of changing tracks. A time to protest to gods. Crying for justice that never came, despite waiting all those years. Is this correct that, "God sees everything but waits", hope came after an year. Again very unexpectedly that sustained me for long. This straw in the troubled waters, I fervently clutched and swam. All my life beset by tragedies and failures, I was always blessed by some saving graces. But this gnawing hopeless times of nearly 2 years, saw me doing other things, I never imagined, I too could do! But never to be repeated again and they are here in a few scores of pages. Never again to be revisited. Turn the pages one at a time; this may not be for a great majority. May be for a hopeless minority, nevertheless, countable. But I never lost either the memories nor my concerns for others.

DEATH OF MY FATHER AND ITS AFTERMATH

In 1964 November my father became very sick from facial paralysis. I had gone to Avidi to attend on him. Of course, I was fearing his ill-health right from 1953-54 when I was in 3rd Form. Medical facilities were meager. Monetary status much worse. Only caste is big – what for? His condition dragged on until now. After seeing me, he recovered greatly, started moving on his own. We all thought he made it again to be amongst us. After a week's stay with him at Avidi village, I returned to Pilani. It took 4 days. On the same day I was informed he became more sick. I moved back. A saga begins which never ended.

As I am traveling home, I knew that my father is no more. I realised this on my reaching Avidi. He was already cremated by my grand father. I was told the events leading to his passing away. He did not die – he was killed by a group of guilty people trying to cover up their crimes by targeting the innocents leadered by one Konda Hanumantha Rao of Jaggannapeta.

Jaggannapeta is a weaver's village. There was a weaver's Co-operative Society, financed and supervised by Konaseema Bank. The Society is closed due to losses, Bank appointed my father as the Supervisor and mandated to report the facts behind the losses. He did. Several Office Bearers were found to have swindled money harming fellow weavers. After the task is over, my father was transferred to another Co-operative Society at Avidi. The criminals facing actions came to Avidi as a group to threaten and counter accuse my father. When he was on bed recouping, these criminals barged into our house and ransacked the room – shouting abuses, cursing, accusing him to have swallowed the money to educate his eldest son somewhere in north, at their expense. All these worsened his health and caused his death after a few days.

Immediately my responsibilities increase, while I am doing research in Rajasthan. How this can be managed. The bank which my father served for 15 years and by my grand father before him, ignored us. They did not give us a gratuity for dying in harness. I requested for some grant from the Common Good Fund. No response. Subsequently they raised salaries retrospectively. But no arrears were paid to us. Some one must have pocketed it signing for him. I requested to give me a Job in the place of my father, on humanitarian grounds. Silence, in-humanism was felt by the office bearers of the bank, who were known to us for years. Most of these belonged to RAJU community known for generosity! I had no money, which is badly needed. I wrote to several friends to send me some. Only a few obliged. The first was Bhaskara Rao.

On my own I started meeting powerful people so as to obtain a lecturer post by next June-July. On one occasion my uncle and me happened to cross each other on road. He was very angry for trying to stop research and obtain a small job. He rebuked me on the road itself. He then asked whether I can send Rs 150 per month instead of Rs 50 now. I said yes. Then he asked me to get back to Pilani and reappear only with a Doctorate. "You send me Rs 150 and I will arrange Rs 50 from my son; and the family will move to Munganda. This man was the husband of my mother's elder sister.

I left for Pilani. I started cooking my food, along with Anand Rao, spent only Rs 80+ out of 250, and sent 150 every month to my family. Mentally, I never recovered from this shock and several shocks from several people. I could not ignore them all.

B V RATNAM AND M C JOSHI

It was 1961. I failed in the SSB interview to become an army officer. I failed in quarterly exams. I was unable to continue studies due to lack of money. Muley sab rescued me. And Dr. B V Ratnam too. He worked in Pilani earlier. Now in Rajasthan Government. He is the Principal of a College. A few months ago, Joshiji took me to Sardar Shahar to meet Ratnam sab. We talked a lot over cups of tea and Bujiya. Ratnam sab gave me a Text of Mycology by Alexopoulos and a text of Botany by Bold. A short, stocky and dusky man from Mori near Antarvedi. He holds the Topper record of BHU in Botany; worked at Pilani, went to USA to work under Kramer on Pine Apples to obtain a Doctorate degree. He was a Jewel. He helped every one. Dr. M C Joshi was very fond of him.

I kept myself aloof from him. I do not know why? I would have got my job in 1967 easily. Prof Ratnam wanted me to marry his daughter and promised to take care of our economic problems. His family offered us 4 acres of Rice fields with 2 crops. The Bollapragada family enjoyed great reputation across generations. I once saw the girl, dark, stout and low in education, this deterred me. My mother was interested in family security. I am confident of the same by my higher education and earnings. And I am fiercely independent in temperament. This made all the difference in life more than once, nay, all the times.

NECESSITY TO BE NEAREST TO MY FAMILY

By December first week, 1964, it was apparent that my father may not lost long. So I began some attempts to get greater income and get nearer to the native place. Prof. Nanda offered me a fellowship at Punjab University in Physiology. But it does not get me any nearer. I wanted to join Prof. Haldane, at Bhubaneswar. When I came to Avidi due to my father's death I read of Haldane's demise in papers. Afterwards I went to Waltair, to ask the HOD, Botany, for a fellowship and placement.

He virtually spurned me! While returning to Pilani I visited Osmania's Botany. I found it decadent and unencouraging. But I found a wise man in Dr. Hashim. My friendship with him continued for decades, a noble man of Genetics. I came back to Pilani, to cook and save Rs 150 for my family.

LETTERS TO ROJA, RELIEF FROM BOREDOM

Roja was my cousin. Our mothers were sisters. She was one of my childhood friends, younger by 3-4 years. Somewhere during mid-1960s, she was passing through a phase in life when she was staying with her brother for studying B.Sc in Reddy's College. The college is boring, and the home much more. She wrote in an inland letter. The reply from me larger. She too wrote a more elaborate letter. The correspondence covered the students, teachers, boys, girls, sometimes their families, their hobbies, ambitions, disappointments, of course not politics. Sometimes we trespassed into crushes, love affairs, romances, dreams and what not. This continued probably for 2-3 years. In 1966 she was married and went away. And the hobby ceased.

Many years later, I happened to visit her, for, her husband too was well known to me. All of a sudden, he said, "thanks a lot, for providing relief to my wife when she was passing stressful times, through your letters. I saw them all, read a few and preserved them". I felt sad for considering them as time-servers rather than builders of ethoses that make up characters and enrich wisdoms.

CULINARY EXERCISES

My father's death necessitated a change in life style and economic measures. When he was alive, I used to send Rs 50/ monthly. Now it has to be raised to Rs 150 from my monthly scholarship of Rs 250. At this time I chanced to meet a student who was about to discontinue studies for want of adequate funds. But he is good in cooking. We then came to a deal – we will live together, sharing the rent. We also cook for ourselves. He cooks and I clean the utensils. Gradually I also learnt making rotis, cooking rice and making Curd! All this costed us Rs 80 per month each. I could easily send Rs 150 home. My companion was Anand Rao from Tumkur of Karnataka, a man par excellence! And this togetherness was catalyzed by Rama Rao, my friend, who happened to be one year senior to Anand Rao.

TELUGUS

Telugu Association grew to have about 40 members by the time I joined as a Research Scholar, from a mere 5, in 1961. They decided to have a facsimile Magazine annually, by name HAARATHI. Its organisation was entrusted to me for some reasons - Hand writing, Pleasantness with people, familiarity with literature, etc. I steered this organ of Telugus for a few years successfully. There were people from many castes and religions, all in harmony. I must record their good will towards me in those times.

In this connection mention must be made of the annual Cultural Week. A notable and exceptional event was the Song of India. All language groups present a Chorus Song in their language depicting their culture. Although a Telugu Song never won a prize during my years there, efforts were always made, very happily by one and all.

At least for a decade the guardian of Telugus was Shri S V N Rao, a faculty of the Electronics Department. He was the permanent president of our association. All students go to him for advices when needed. Any one facing problems, necessarily go to him and many times he was successful in helping. He was a voracious reader and conversationalist. I have learnt a good deal of history from him. He was very good to all of us and helpful.

The other notable person, joined during my time there, in Chemical Engineering was Dr. K.S. Rao from Andhra University. He was good in teaching and research, very knowledgeable, culture conscious and progressive– an euphemism for being pro-communistic. We naturally became very good friends - very genuine. He was collecting R K Lakshman's cartoons; used to discuss current affairs and Andhra cultural scene, very frequently, sometimes daily. A very rare man - we do not come across easily.

SURENDRA BABU, RAMA RAO AND PRANAB RAY

There are other contributing factors to my growth. First and most significant was Surendra Babu my contemporary from Physics Department was an excellent human and a teacher to whom I owe a lot. Among others, he introduced two books – Saagutunna Yatra and Smruti Padhamlo by Achanta Janakiram.- The Continuing Journey and Down the Memory Line. The first one narrated the author's travels and experiences. The second one dealt with his reflections and introspections after settling down. These recollections mostly tell us our foolish talks, deeds, and make us imagine "I should have done like this" or "I should not have" – all from hindsight wisdom. It is really not a settled, but the most turbulent time in the mind.

These two phases are inevitable in everyone's life. These made me reflect as I move and see in others what many did not! And more, I did not see what was obvious for many! My mind and heart always remained turbulent while on journey as well as in my current sanctuary of retirement. I am indebted to Surendra Babu and Janaki Ram. As a token I became instrumental in getting these two books reprinted, bearing most of the expenditure, under the auspices of Jyeshtha Literary Trust in Vishakhapatnam. The revenue of over a lakh of rupees was given to the writer 'Bharago,' who was ailing. It was however not acknowledged in the reprint. So much for values even among the old stalwarts, in these market times.

After he has left came Ramarao, a younger brother of Shri S V N Rao. It was a great pleasure to listen to him, a great conversationalist at that young age, I owe him my introduction to Telugu Literature, Communists, Current National and International Politics. Next came a savior,

Anandarao, who became my room mate, cooked food for ourselves, to save Rs 150 per month so as to enable me send it to my family at home. Finally came Pranab Ray, an all time influence over me. Without all these people I would have remained only a raw commoner!

SANJEEV DEV AND JANAKIRAM

A very memorable experience during my stay in Pilani were the articles by Sanjeevadev and by Janakiram. The former were published as a book later –as Rasare-khalu. Achanta Janakiram, son of a Titan in Ayurveda – Ayurveda Bhishagvara Achanta Lakshmipati – wrote articles which later became two books –Sagutunna Yatra and Na Smrutipadhamlo.

I felt that every one must read Janakiram. From here I believed that every one will have a story of the self, and must be recorded for posterity. Interestingly both these authors wrote in a paper edited by Narla Venkateswara Rao – My favourite Journalist and thinker. His articles on Lokam Pokada are a must-read.

PRANAB'S FRIENDS

Because of Pranab, I used to go to my home town in Andhra via Kolkata. There were three memorable experiences. One was the invigorating atmosphere in the entire college street. The second was the depressing sight of women in the red light area that we had to witness on way to Rabindra Bharathi, Tagore's House. The third is the periodical gathering of friends of Pranab near his house in the Railway Colony to discuss the current political situation.

Ashim Chatterjee: A first class first in both Physics and Chemistry M.Sc of Calcutta University was a regular, along with many later day prominent communists. He is widely respected even today by all leftists. In one of our meetings a great concept emerged on the contiguity of hills, forests and people from Bihar to Northern Andhra so as to establish the routes of passage for future usage. The current connectivity among the revolutionaries from Nepal to Southern Andhra was the result of his pioneering work conceptualised in our meetings then! And Trotsky's Cretinism that plagued both Lenin and Mao, was defeated by this approach. Ashim used to tell that all people cannot do all things but each must do what one can do for the good of others. I was happy to be associated with the emergence of this concept.

ORIGIN OF BUSINESS MANAGEMENT

Business Administration as a subject was borne here. Dr. Dool Singh, Professor of Commerce, went to USA under the BITS -MIT Programme. He came a completely changed man in many respects. Many new faculty were recruited. Syllabi changed, admission rules altered. In just one year we found changes in faculty, students and their programmes. These students started behaving as if they are different from others and superior, even in speech and attire. This department was one of the earliest ones in India in this subject.

LOCAL HOSPITALITY

At Pilani, a classmate of mine, Jayant Kumar Gupta, frequently used to take me to his house in town, to enjoy conversations and food, Bujiya and Tea. His father was an ADC to the President of India. Another person was Mr. Shekhawat, a budding artist and my student then. He also often took me to his house for a sumptuous Rajput Lunch or Dinner. He was the son of the famous artist, a childhood friend of G D Birla, whose paintings adorned the offices of Birla's Establishments, all over India.

Although I do not wish to highlight my financial problems, helps were rendered to me by others from time to time, are only God-sent. In both the summer vacations, I was given the task of assisting Prof. Muley in tabulating Marks of students of Rajasthan University. The stipend was enough to live, travel to home in Andhra and return. This was done in 1962 and 1963. In 1963 July, authorities created a post of Museum Assistant for my sake. Then recommended me for a Doctoral fellowship, which I enjoyed for 3 years. After the completion of this term, I was given a Temporary Lecturership, in the leave vacancy, caused by the departure of Prof. Pillai to USA.

My professors obtained me three jobs elsewhere telling that my family needed more income and on permanent basis. But I told mummyji, I want to be like my guru, my Professor, a Doctorate and an Oxbridge Professor like him. These posts were given to my own classmates, on my recommendation – to KNS Nair, Raghunandanan and

Devendra Mohan Kapoor. I always tried to become a Babu Narhar Muley.

FOREIGNERS

When I joined Pilani there were only two foreigners. Prof. Wendel teaching German and French, and Prof. Lewis was in English department. The former is more popular for his interests in literature and history and the Library-cum-Museum he maintains in his house. But he is fond of students and tirelessly tried to impart interests in his favourite subjects. Another interest was Current Affairs, Prof. Lewis is a very private person outside his department, probably harbours strong opinions on India.

Seasons change: Americans arrive from MIT. Prof. Drew, a Chemical Engineer and Prof. Baker of Social Sciences, moved around, met people, conversed, attended Seminars and coolly left after spending a semester or two. Then came Cyrus Levinthal a Molecular Biologist of international repute, working on Genes and DNA. He spent probably a week, talked with as many biology people as possible, left comments, attended my convocation and finally was unsatisfied with the scenario here. He was explicit about everything.

The Russian Lady teaches Russian.

LOTHAR WENDEL

Last but not the least, the greatest saving grace of BITS, Pilani, is Lothar Wendel. Most people in the campus considered him and me as close friends. Yes I was the closest to him, because most people used to avoid him as plague for their own reasons or non-reasons. He used to invite people to his house but rarely any one ever entertained him. He is not a person disliked, but one who is not understood.

Wendel was from Damstadt, a small town in Germany. He was a Lieutenant in the German Army during the 2nd World War. While on the eastern front, he was caught by the Russians. He was in Russian captivity for 6 years in Leningrad, today's Petersburg. Daily they were made to march in the streets there with rifles, butts up and heads down. From here, he was released under the armistice.

From here to Pilani the journey,
he never talked to me,
nor answered me!

He was teaching us German and French, as the students choose. A Foreign language is compulsory for all research scholars as part of the Ph.D programme. Russian was the other. This is how me, Sushma Nanda, Ambuja Pillai used to attend his classes every evening for an year. We preferred German and fared creditably.

He was always longing for company, suffering from loneliness, a kind of imprisonment, solitary. With two deaths behind me, I understood his predicaments tried to satisfy him to the extent possible. Whenever invited, I always went to his house. Whatever he talked I listened although unintelligible. He got Pranab, Pillai, Subba Rao etc through me to converse and take tea with. His house was the last in his row, after which there are no more houses. He goes about by a cycle. Occasionally stops here and there either for a black tea or for smoking a cigarette, of Red & White brand. Everywhere he was a sight.

He would always take the black milk-less tea! He revels in vaxing eloquent about Europe, Adenauer, De Gaulle, East-West Detante and a separate European vision away from Anglo-American outlook. This philosophy is understood in his house, which is a museum of the world in the eyes of Europe. I have gone through this museum several times – each time a part.

It is here I have learnt of Max Mueller and Herman Keserling. I am told and later I read about the revolt of soldiers at Munich. I vividly read about the attempt of Count Stauffenberg to assassinate Hitler by a bomb. Years before the cinema. Many authors and philosophers were introduced to me through their works – Thomas Mann, Herman Hesse, Arthur Kostler, Bertholt Brecht. Among the French, Camus, Sartre, Simon de Bouvre, Andre Mourio, Boudelaire, he would tell us about all these people briefly. Except his kitchen and bedroom the entire space was filled by items of his interest.

About this house and people in touch by him he brought out a book namely, German Civilisation at Pilani. For which I was made to write a suitable Poem kept as Appendix. This was in 1968! I lost touch with him after I left BITS and then North India in 1969.

He presented me with a book of poetry, in German on one side and in English on the opposite page. One of my favourite poems was:

I am on a horse carriage
I do not like the place I am going to
I do not like the place from where I am coming
The driver stopped the carriage
He is changing the wheel
Why am I still sitting in the cart?

This period with Prof. Wendel was a part of my education, unforgettable!

OTHER INFLUENCES

With the inheritance from two grand fathers – one an Innocent Congressman, another a wise Reformist of Literary leanings, my college background, I am easily given to sensitivity despite all disadvantages of remoteness to the mainstream communications, poverty and false pride of a Brahmin society, I survived and moved only with the help of innumerable good men and women. I was lucky to be born in Gandhian times, and to have studied during Nehruvian times, when Humanism was still an important trait, now a rare commodity.

After Blitz and Karanzia during my college days, I was influenced at Pilani by NOW, edited by Humayun Kabir. Later it became FRONTIER under the editorship of a Bengali Poet, Samar Sen. I gave the back issues of these journals to Prof. Amulya Reddy of Indian Institute of Science, Bangalore. He was a good old friend of mine during my years at the Indian Institute of Science. Those three memorable years at Bangalore vanished like three days!

Thus, I was exposed to many authors and books such as Premchand, Mulkraj Anand, Khwaja Abbas, Sadat Manto, RK Narayan, Pearl Buck, Somerset Maugham, Herman Hesse, Andre Maurios, Ayn Rynd, Wol Soyinka, James Baldwin, Bertholt Brecht, and greatly influenced by all–ultimately confused! In Telugu, Ranganayakamma, Sri Sri, Gopichand were my favourites. Naturally I became useless in worldly matters and any one could mislead and cheat me which happened all my life. Since these backgrounds are generally absent in most around us, misunderstanding me became a norm, to my detriment. Some poems, mostly on women, were inspired by books – Bachelor of Arts, Siddhardha, Inquilab, Untouchable, to mention a few. These were facilitated by the library which was representative of India and books were carefully selected. I used to be such a regular reader that I was included in the Library Committee by the authorities, a great honour in those days!

I learnt here that sufferings are not limited to me and spread in society, which made me one in the suffering milieu. This outlook gradually turned me into a socialist and ultimately a Marxist. Most others think conversely and become self-centered, while I identified with the sufferings of others. This made all the difference in later life.

HOW I IMPROVED MY ENGLISH AND WHY?

Within a few days of my stay in the hostels, department and campus, I realised it is a world of English of Hindi people. I was not discouraged. As a student of Blitz at Amalapuram, I thought there is a chance to improve myself. First I maintained a notebook of words I see in newspapers whose meaning I did not know. I worked in the library to get their meanings. This helped in understanding the journalistic language. Second, I opened a notebook with a green judicial paper to write notes about every book I read, a habit, I developed during college times. It was full of Telugu books initially. Gradually giving way to English. The authors I have heard of in blitz during college times, I see their books in the library at Pilani. Thus, my initial readings were Pearl Buck, RK Narayan, Mulk Raj Anand, KA Abbas, Maugham. From all these I made notes, key words, phrases and sentences, quotations, etc. Then is the problem of pronunciations. I used to go to the terrace in the evening with a newspaper, read loudly the editorial more than once. If by chance, I come across interesting material, take it to the top of building and read aloud – no records, no one to tell an opinion. This continued without any monitoring of improvement as it is not possible. The improvement became visible in some debating competition –where others expressed opinions, freely. This continued for a few years, probably until 1965. Until people used to come to me for assistance in drafting or correcting scripts.

PANDITJI'S TEETAR JOINT AND A BRAHMIN MUTTON PARTY

There is no non-vegetarian food in Pilani. Those who desire it adopt various methods. Hotels also are discouraged. One ingenious one opened a small joint serving a small local bird only. They are limited depending on the catch and served for only those who bring their rotis, so that he could concentrate on the bird cooking! The bird is called Teetar, whose song is believed to be a bad omen and is supposed to be afraid of Krishna, the boy.

Many of us found this convenient except for the rotis, because it is impossible to get them around the time Panditji begins to cook the birds. Panditji, is from the hills, a Pahadi. Every one failed to get rotis. Then I tried. I asked the Pahadis at the mess of Ram and Buddha Bhavans. They obliged but asked to collect the rotis before the mess opens. So I did the same, go to the Joint and wait for others to come to enjoy a very delicious dish. Thus, everything cannot be managed as per our desires. Some innovations and extra efforts are needed.

For long I was considered a vegetarian. It was true. My professor and warden Dr. Deshpande, challenged whether I will begin eating mutton. I said Why Not Sir? What about cleaning the mutton ? I agreed even for this. The Pahadi Chowkidar brought the mutton and both of us cleaned it. Thus, I cleaned the stuff first and eaten later. I never learnt cooking, however! By around 11 AM guests started arriving. It was a great shock because all of them were Brahmins! And the cooking was by a Brahmin when his wife has gone home in Maharashtra. Rotis came from the Hostel mess. This was the occasion I have eaten one of the best mutton curries ever !

LOOSING A LECTURER POST

I have not always behaved intelligently despite having it enough. One such was regarding the lecturer post in my department. Since I was the only local candidate, I was very confident of getting it although I did not yet get the doctorate. And I missed the post. It took 6 turbulent years to get a similar Lecturer post. Had I just tried a bit for this post, made some efforts, now I feel I would have got it. I could have personally meet Joshiji at home and requested him to help. I could have met the Director Lakshminarayanan sought his blessings. I should have requested Prof. Ratnam to intervene here. This is the most major mistake I did in my life which had terrible consequences on many. This is due to over confidence? Arrogance? Vanity? Lack of foresight? I think all.

JAYASREE TEA GARDENS - MONEY VS CONTENTMENT

I am in great need of money. This can come only by good employment. This is known to my professor and Mummyji well. When I returned to Pilani after the vacation of 1963, Muley sab got me a lecturer job at Rohtak College. But I declined and got it for Nair, my class mate. I already failed to enter army having exhausted both my chances in the SSB. Then Mummyji got me a post of Assistant Manager in Jayasree Tea Gardens in Assam. Professor asked me to go due to heavy salary [Rs 400 pm]. I declined this too and sent D M Kapoor, my another classmate. Then they asked "what do you want ?" My reply: "I want to obtain Ph. D and become like Professor". There was a silence and we all parted. Immediately he gave me a job of Museum Assistant with a salary of Rs 150. After 2 months he recommended for the post of Research Scholar to do Ph.D. The stipend is just Rs 250 pm for 3 years.

MUNGANDA AT PILANI

Many times I stayed at Delhi with KDP Rao, a research scholar in zoology. He was from my adopted village, Munganda, known to me in the college. He was my junior. I was indirectly responsible for his coming to Pilani, and directly in getting a seat in Zoology M.Sc. despite his failure once in B.Sc. His family has a camaraderie with me. Many times I was Prasadam's guest at Delhi University, in Gwyer Hall, Jubilee Hall enjoying free lunches and dinners. For some unknown reason, he had distanced himself from me, as time passed.

There was yet another before him, from the same village, SMM Rao, a cousin from my mother's side. He too obtained a seat at Pilani, in M.Tech despite his failure in M.Sc once, due to my good offices with Prof. Chaudhary of Electronics. He was much against KDP Rao's coming. I achieved an impossible success in getting him, a failed candidate, a seat! Instead of remaining ever grateful, he indulged in betrayal, due to which I suffer even today. Jealousy, envy and vengeance towards one's benefactors was not common in those times. For helping this Mohan Rao I exceeded all limits. This made up his career, his life. He afflicted my marital life by unnecessary talking and he distroyed my family life with mother, siblings and relatives through silence. Confronted, he admitted to have taken revenge for ignoring him on some occasion while dealing with some Labour strike. Had I done as he wanted, he would have been dismissed from service at BITS.

BHASKAR RAO AND BABU RAO COULD NOT BE HELPED

It was easier to get a seat to Prasadam in M.Sc Zoology compared to Mohan Rao in M.Tech, for he failed in M.Sc. Physics. We had to adopt illegal and illegitimate methods just to make his career and life. He never wanted to go to Hyderabad again to be under the umbrella of his brothers. I got a seat to my classmate in Amalapuram, Bhaskara Rao easily, but he could not join here due to family pressures. He has to be at Sirpur Khagaznagar, and support his younger sisters in their education and upbringing. Another disappointment was Babu Rao, another relative and friend from Munganda Agrahaaram. He also first failed in B. Sc, but never completed. He opted to bow to family pressures, marry in the same village and be happy ever after.

MY DOCTORAL THESIS

My doctoral work and thesis has an interesting story to reveal until the convocation. I had a great jolt when my father died and I had to support my family in 1964 December – 14 months into the fellowship. I was saved by my uncle, husband of my mother's sister. I received another shock a year after when my professor passed away. And no one wants to be the official supervisor unless I change my topic. I did not want to change to Ecology, as Dr. Joshi was unserious about science and manipulates data. All others are morphologists, a subject whose value has waned. Since I was sent to Dr. M.S. Swaminathan, by my Professor, I wanted to continue with my current research problem. Dr. Deshpande, another benefactor, became my official supervisor, on the grounds of humanism. I continued my work.

After some time, I faced a block, some thing like a writer's block. Prof. D K. Santra of Pharmacy happened to return from USA at that time and came to know of my predicaments. He was very fond of me and in fact wanted to take me under his guard. But I had to change the field to Pharmacognacy. He called me and asked me to test FIVE chemicals, all alkaloids, just extracted from some plants and gifted to him by the US Scientist, Gardon Svoboda, from Lily Research Laboratories. I did. Initial results were fantastic, which came just in one week. Dr. Santra asked me to test all and put the results in the thesis. And this work became a great chapter of my thesis.

The thesis was prepared in Dr. Deshpande's house. I was regularly corrected by Prof. Pillai, my yet another benefactor. Some data are not yet ready on chromosome measurements. Sankara Reddy, a definitive man, a Research Scholar from zoology helped me in this completion with in time – a significant timely help. When the thesis was ready with the help of so many students, a procession of 15-20 Botany students carried the 4 copies of thesis to the registrar and submitted. It was 30, October 1968. We got the positive result from the examiners before the end of January. Then rules changed. Viva Voce had to be open as desired by the American Advisors. In mid-February, the first open Viva Voce, with all Faculty and Students of Botany, and allied departments, was conducted by the TWO examiners for about an Hour. I received all round appreciation.

Convocation was in March. Six people were awarded the Doctorates by Shri G D Birla and Dr. Dharma Vira, the then Governor of West Bengal. And this was televised by the Developers of it, Central Electronic Engineering Research Institute, for the first time in India.

ETHICS IN SCIENCE

I experienced a variety of people overwhelmingly good and forthcoming. But I also saw negative aspects occasionally which tended to dominate with the passage of time. In my MSc, I was working in Grassland Ecology for a thesis. I thought of doing a Doctorate too. But I changed my field due to a fact I saw. The teacher is manipulating data and asked us to follow. For leaving him, he later punished me by rejecting me in the interview for lecturer post there!

In the same Institution, the Zoology Professor asked me to teach Cytology Techniques to the M.Sc students and later classes. In the history of BITS I was the only teacher who taught in two departments, - Genetics, both in Botany as well as in Zoology, and creditably. That was a spirit. I was allowed by Pharmacy Department to attend classes in Chromatography and Microbiology. Their Professor Dr. Santra, obtained for me some rare chemicals from USA. A cytological technique was applied to a desert reptile. The result was published by me and the zoology research Scholar, Surendra Singh. This happened to be the first report of chromosome number. When he told to his Professor, he called me and appreciated openly. I enjoyed enormous goodwill not only in botany but also in Zoology, Chemistry and Pharmacy – this became a habit with others, later a culture.

During my tenure, the scripts of completed work were used to be sent to Dr. A K Koul, a lecturer at Rajasthan University, Jaipur. He was a Teacher to my colleague Avtar Singh on whose suggestion I took this chance. Dr. Koul meticulously corrected my scripts and our friendship flourished for decades – me considering him my GURU.

Science was a serious affair during Nehruvian times, we following Haldane Principles which continued all my life and as a plague in this current society. Dr. Gundu Rao and Professor Santra, laterly Dr. M.S. Swaminathan's colleagues – AT Natarajan, HK Jain, BC Joshi, RK Sharma, Pai, Chanchal Kapoor, Amar Singh, Prof. Ramdas Menon – I learnt Science and began to admire Darwin, Huxley, Muller. I arrived into the field of Science, whose ingredients never left me, just as the literary and political interests, to this day. I believe these are still alive within me.

SCIENTIFIC ATTITUDES - VINCA AND CANNABIS

I got my Ph.D in 1969 for a thesis submitted in 1968. One of the Indian Examiners was a professor from Delhi University. In the viva voce examination he praised the work with Vinca alkaloids. In 1971, when I joined the Indian Institute of Science at Bangalore, I found a research paper on the same subject by him ! And there was no mention of our work either in the introduction, or in the references or in the acknowledgments. Then I remembered my work on Cannabis while working in M.S. Swaminathan's laboratory. When N.P. Sarma told me of his similar work and showed, I found it far better than mine. I encouraged him to publish it and I withdrew mine. He probably acknowledged my role. These two events demonstrate the changing values in scientific research.

ABSENCE OF MENTORING AND KOTIREDDY

It did not come to my mind at all at this time that going to US to get a doctorate there would have earned me enough cash to fend my family here. Unlike others, I did not take this route. I also did not try for competitive Central Services as some believed that my good general knowledge and English would have made me successful. But I was enamored by a doctorate degree, a rarity in those days. I wished to be like my Professor, Babu Narhar Muley! Teachers were not advising students on their intellectual labours, not helping them in taking correct decisions. This was pointed out many times by a graduate student, Avuthu Kotireddy, who used to be fond of me for several reasons. One of them was mentoring. He used to ask me plenty of questions. I could satisfy him to some extent. He used to confess that he is most satisfied, only with me!

NCC FOR ALL DURING 1962-3

When I was in the second year of M.Sc Chinese invaded India. This had many consequences. One such was the compulsion of NCC for all in Pilani. But where is the manpower to run the machine ? One of the resource persons the administration found was me. Before coming to Pilani, I passed Certificate 'C' and was an Under Officer. I further faced the Services Selection Board for direct recruitment as an Officer. Thus, the mantle fell on me to organise. Organising the Post graduate students into files, ranks, squads, platoons and companies, teaching them drill. Of all the toughest is to inculcate a dress sense, punctuality and quietitude. This phase continued for 4 months during 1963. Most people in the hostels used to call me Ustadji !

CHAMPIONS WITHOUT TROPHIES

During this time I won the Championship of the Carrom Board. This was a surprise. Became a reality because some better players did not contest for their reasons. At BITS the championships in every conceivable sports and games are common for Students, Research Scholars and Faculty. In Carrom Doubles, thus me and my Research Guide, Dr. Deshpande became the

Champions. But we did not get trophies, but mere certificates due to the war situation in the borders !

MUTTON SOUP FOR A MONTH

For some time, I fell ill due to Gastro-enteritis and became very weak. Taking any vitamins and tonics of sorts were of no avail. Dr. Choksi then prescribed to take bone marrow soup for a month. But this is not possible because non-vegetarian foods were not allowed in the campus. Then as a last resort we went to the Birla Education Trust Secretary, Dr. Pandeji and put our predicament before him.

He then summoned the Manager of a small hotel, Volga and had a talk with the Hospital. After ascertaining the facts, he ordered the hotel to give me marrow soup every day in the evening around 6-7 PM for one month and some exercises to me and report back to him after the end of this period.

This was the first time that Non-Veg food, though at a very small scale was introduced at BITS Campus.

PROF. MORRIS OF CHINCHINADA UNIVERSITY, CANADA

A research scholar in Botany was judged adversely by several colleagues in the hostel, for reasons now forgotten. They hatched a harmless conspiracy against him that ran nearly for 6 months. The scholar was AKK, some 3 years junior to me. I had no role except enjoying the fun. The leader of the whole fun was our research guide, Dr. Deshpande, who is also our warden. AKK was working on the wood anatomy of some legumes. Most of them had to be collected from various parts of India and some from other countries. AKK wrote letters to many scientists, including some from Canada, not realising that temperate countries are unlikely to support plants necessary for his research that focuses on tropical and subtropical climes. So a letter was written by him to Prof. Morris of Chinchinada University, Canada but posted by Trivedi, his senior. A reply was arranged by Ramakrishna of Zoology. The key man in the whole episode is the post man. Next time it was posted by some other scholar. Replies from Morris were drafted by Deshpandeji. Morris would periodically write appreciating his work, always promising to send material after collecting it from various sources. Packages with wood also started coming. They are all collected locally by his friends. Interestingly Chinchinada happened to be the native place of Ramakrishna in Andhra. One day Deshpandeji told them all to close this soon. One day a big package of legumes came from Dr. Morris. Ashok was too happy and announced that he would work hard, day and night and complete Ph.D sooner than his seniors. As soon as people demanded a party, he immediately agreed and gave it in the Cafeteria to a dozen hilarious research scholars of Botany and Zoology and the post man, where the joke was busted by Deshpandeji. Ashok too took it very sportively.

SEASON FOR CUPID

So as to satisfy human curiosities I try to be more

explicit. Many girls entered my company due to departmental proximities and the residential nature of the institution. Mutual crushes develop naturally. I had crush on girls here and there as it is the urge of the youth. My crushes remained unexpressed. Others had crush on me – also untold. By and large, they were all passing birds without a song or passing clouds without a rain to make us wet, except one.

I was asked to take classes after my professor's death. Fortunately became a popular teacher and trainer in Practical exercises. The reputation spread to Zoology Department. Prof. Datta Gupta asked me to take classes for them too. Because my subject – Cytogenetics was a paper in both Botany and Zoology. My class used to have thus the biggest strength in science departments, over 30, with 15-20 girls. Students like good teachers, more so the girls. I was a center of attraction for many girls, though I was not aware. All life I continued to be innocent about the fair sex. But a few girls made them transparent. It was my friends and a cousin, who later betrayed, used to tease me of. Some embarrassing situations too I faced and solved with their help.

But I could not resist one, Sheela and started falling quietly; then openly after leaving BITS, which resulted in cataclysmic events which broke me permanently. I was never again the man with such promise my friends and teachers anticipated at BITS, Pilani and IISc at Bangalore. This was a combination of failure and tragedy. Failures are mine, but the tragedies brought into my life undeservingly, are also mine; and the individuals perpetrating them are close people, unforgivable and unforgettable! I considered them from the social context but those hey days of popularity at BITS produced some romantic pieces, never again to be experienced, either platonically or really.

I fell for one encouraged by my cousin, Mohan Rao and a friend, Subba Rao. It became serious because it was sincere. It helped both for a while. It improved her and her grades. And it made me complete my thesis. This led us to marriage in the months to come and break in the times of stress! This forever remained a tragedy that never healed in my life.

Permissiveness increased due to the American Academic Tourism. There was an atmosphere of romance and a free for all in the air, but sporadically. All these are drizzles, not rains. During my time, there were only some girls who can be called beauties.

Some I remember. Santosh Rastogi, Mallika Bhattacharya, Harminder Kaur, Archana Goel, Prem Arora, Deepika Mehta, Padmini Nair. Miss. Awalgaonkar is the best of all. Daughter of Chief of the Hospital, a Maharashtrian, used to accompany her parents. They always attended all functions in Botany as friends of our Professor Muley. She was very cultured with regal bearing. Invariably there will be a song by her. Even now, decades later, I remember her singing "Hamari Yad Ayegi..." by Mubarak Begum.

However, beauty lies in the beholder. The love affairs of those times did not involve any of them; but strange combinations came on stage! Surendra Singh and his Jaswant Kaur, Arun Goel and another Sikh girl, Vanasree Tiwari and her Boy friend, Neelam Ahuja and Cricketer Sharma, Jayant Gupta and Usha Tolani, Upadyaya and Kamalesh Tanwar, Uma Chawla and Sharma, Narendra Babu and Rajeswari, Sadhana and Rao, Sheela and Sharma, etc, some pairs remembered. In memory because, many girls were in my classes. Some suitors were known to me. For some I wrote love letters on their behalf. Needless to say most girls are from Botany and Zoology and men from Engineering. Some eloped. Some ended in marriages. Some failed. Some broken by hostile families. I was a witness to one poignant story. The man who failed continued to be my friend for decades!

The triumph, as it looked like first gradually turned out to be a tragedy all through my life. When a step is put forward it was not evident that two steps will go backward. The entire life became star-crossed but consolation comes from Bhishma's stoic Philosophy in Mahabharata, of late. Only this much is willed!

Mohanrao used to sit in my room, while I was demonstrating practicals to students, and watch the girls and found one of them had different, admiring looks towards me. So he advised, I proposed and succeeded. We used to meet every Saturday afternoon in his official chamber in electronics department. His eldest brother Sitarama Sastry, warned us earlier that plans are going on to marry both of us to two sisters – in – law of Gopalam, and keep us under control. We opposed his dictatorial methods and rebelled. I was accused of his marriage, when

I had no role. But because of them all, my marital life was greatly damaged!

MY BIGGEST REGRET

I could not reward Peddi to express my gratitude. She was beaten to death by her son for her action of heart, a philanthropy to me. She never appeared in my house, in our street, anywhere else. But the entire village remembered her for decades. And I never forgot her, but for her, I could have never made it to Pilani and higher studies.

MIGRAINE AND ALLERGIES

I have been a patient of migraine since the age of 10. Suffering has been inexplicable. At Pilani, its frequency has been low. Once I got it while doing Professor's work at his home in summer. Mummyji made me lie on the bed and massaged Amrutanjan on my forehead and summoned the doctor from the hospital. That is the care never forgotten. Although migraine became less severe, I seem to have developed allergies and more sensitive to smells. I was allergic to petrol, cocoanut oil, smell of Sandal, Agarbatti. At the same time my pains reduce with the smell of lemon and lemon based perfumes or heavy sneezing!

JHUNJHUNU COURT WITH MULEY SAB

In those times one is selected by the central government for a scholarship to get a Ph.D. A legal bond to return the money in case one discontinues, was necessary. When I was awarded in 1963 September, I faced the problem of surety. One fine morning Professor called me and said we are going to Jhunjhunu. We both boarded the car and reached the court. In front of the Magistrate, he signed as the surety. We returned. Nothing was talked. This has never happened. No Professor ever stood surety for a research scholar. This news astonished people in the department and other neighbouring ones. The affection and trust shown by mummyji and Professor was without a parallel and what made them judge me trustworthy remained one of the mysteries of my life.

EASHWARI KHUSHALANI AND AMBUJA PILLAI

Normally I was available to all in the department for various assistances I am capable of. I was surprised when Easwariji asked me to do a correction work of her thesis that was returned for reviewing by the examiners. I agreed, thoughtlessly. The work was tough in all respects, for one has to go through each line find out errors in punctuations, spellings, in the minimum. And my own knowledge was inadequate. Sitting in Prof. Pillai's Laboratory, I gave her back some pages in the forenoon and some more in the afternoon. Efficiency increased. My knowledge improved. The whole department was astonished and appreciated for the positive attitude of a student.

After some time the same happened, for Mrs. Ambuja Pillai. The same type of work, with a difference. This time it was before submission. And the examiner appreciated the care the student took in making her thesis error - free!

SOME INCIDENTS DURING RESEARCH TENURE

When my father died and Professor became sick, he gave me a letter and sent me to Delhi to meet M S Swaminathan. I did and it helped me a lot in later years. At Pilani also I kept all my senses open, which opened several avenues open for progress. We one day dissected a desert lizard and found two mini balls. Ramakrishna and Surendra Singh identified them as ovaries. I thought why not we subject it Feulgen test and see what is there. If the balls are ovaries, it could produce eggs, if eggs are produced, there must be meiosis; when meiosis occurs chromosomes will be visible. Why not take a chance to look for these? We got bivalents, one of which was asymmetrical. Thus, we found out, by chance and curiosity, the chromosome number of a desert lizard, Acanthodactylus cantoris cantoris. And the asymmetrical pair is of the sex-chromosomes. This was a first finding. This led to teaching some chromosome related practicals with Drosophila; later, theory classes etc in Zoology department.

I stumbled upon Pranab Ray, by chance probably due to Prafulla, his class mate. I was so much impressed by him that our friendship never ceased but grew.

I soon found myself auditing Microbiology and Chromatography classes along with M. Pharm Students. I practised chromatography, paper and TLC - both ascending and descending. An idea to probe germinated. We screened fertile and sterile seeds of Ephedra foliata for free amino acids. And got some meaningful results. Pharmacy Professor Dr. Santra was so much impressed by my attitudes and approaches that he wished to take me in his research scheme on turmeric, but could not happen for some interdepartmental reasons. Dr. Gundu Rao became a consultant and confidante for all of us. I chanced to meet both Santra and Rao in Odisha and Manipal, respectively. Great collaborations! With Pranab Ray our actions took many wings. Haldane conference was one that did not take place.

On his death anniversary, we took Prof J B S Haldane as an icon of youth with scientific spirit. We brought out a pamphlet - me, Pranab and Pillai, his classmate. It was well received and appreciated. We felt encouraged to start a Haldane Society and organise a conference of like minded people for promoting scientific attitude and temper. But this became a great failure, mostly because of lack of experience as well as guidance.

All other activities are in some stage of progress. Yet the main work of mine is always related to my doctoral research. One aspect of my work involves collection of material round the clock, for 24 hours, once a month. We had difficulties in collecting in winter months. Now it became less difficult. Pranab brought a Railway Overcoat of his father, to protect ourselves in the winter months. Ananda Rao of zoology or Pranab would accompany me to the field with a vials of fixative every hour – the difficult hours being the midnight to morning hours in winter months. The security first observed us, next questioned and reported last. The matter was taken to Professors Pillai, Datta Gupta and Santra. We were summoned by them and appreciated. The director, Prof. Lakshminarayanan, as stern as K N Singh of Indian Cinema, chided for not taking prior permission.

These results were neither included in the thesis nor published separately as we had to abandon this work due to a psychological depression I underwent due to the injustice meted out to me by Dr. M C Joshi, my another teacher which was not resisted by any one.

FANCIES AND TIT-BITS

Doing something all the time has become a culture developing. Thus, for some time I surveyed Ephedra foliata and found that the seeds are very variable, polymorphic. Association with pharmacy department prompted me to use chromatography on them. We found that the free aminoacids were different in these seeds. I was excited. But how to confirm and go further. I had to abandon.

Then I found that 2 grasses are very interesting in their habit depending on their habitats. I wanted to characterise them. They turned out to be ecotypes. These works were never published because they are never completed. Manipulating data never entered my system, for it is immoral but indulged by one teacher Dr. M.C. Joshi. These grasses are Cenchrus and Dactyloctenium. They are autecologies. A little more work would have fetched me a doctorate and also a job. Because Dr. Joshi wanted that way to score over others through me, but quietly advocating data manipulations. I refused and he denied the lecturership, to get which elsewhere a struggle for 6 more years was the price!

Blitz in those days was publishing articles on South America, Amazon and those people especially the head-hunters. And I found many books in our library on these subjects. They were very interesting. Then began a phase of discovering South America. Why ? Any Utility ? only curiocity! Daily I was reading these books one after another and making notes. A huge information piled up written in my own hand. I do not know what happened to this bulk. Love's labour lost!

MURALIDHARAN, THE PALMIST

In zoology department there was a student by name Muralidharan. He had a reputation for being a good Palmist. Almost all research scholars in the hostel used to engage him. I did not do. During later years I chanced to meet him at Ahmedabad in the university where he was working for his Doctorate. I asked him of Palmistry. He confessed that it is a matter of a psychology of a personality, social status, worries, desires, hopes and fears – They need to be carefully mixed and told. Sometimes the candidates reveal themselves. He requested me not to tell any one that he is a palmist, lest they do not allow him to do his work.

POROUS RCC

Pranab, Pillai and Me brought out a Pamphlet of about 8 pages on J B S Haldane on his death Anniversary. It was widely appreciated. So was the booklet Wiseacres by Mehta, an engineering student already famous as the brother of Deepika Mehta, a beauty from the Pharmacy Department. Then came an interesting scandal. A porous RCC, in the First Floor. I was responsible for this. After working in the night I forgot to close a tap and left for hostel. Next morning I was woken up and summoned to the Department of Botany. I found the floor full of water. As if not enough it was percolating to the department below, Zoology. The concrete with which floors are made are never known to be porous until then. This technology is worthy of wide publicity, we felt then. Authorities felt differently. A secret of theirs, lay bared.

PADMINI'S UNIQUE BEAUTY

A student of zoology from Kerala, Padmini is one of the beautiful girls on the campus during my time. Nay. She is the most beautiful girl because she has a look of piety. A divine look. She appears as a goddess. Any goddess. A rare feature. Probably she is the person having maximum suitors after her. But she did not budge or waver even a bit. She left Pilani with the same simplicity she carried on arrival!

THE EPIC JOURNEY FOR NOTHING

I submitted my thesis for the award of a PhD on 30 October 1968, just a day before the deadline. It was nothing short of a miracle. No one expected I would do. Many people were happy.

Immediately, I took the bus to Loharu and then a train to Delhi. From the same station took the earliest train towards Howrah, until Assansol. Then there was a passenger to Cuttack. I boarded that and disembarked at post midnight at Kendrapara Road station. I found to my surprise that the town is 30 km away. Luckily I got a Taxi which I hired both ways. A lonely windy pleasant journey to Kendrapara town. Just to show my achievement of a Doctoral thesis to my lady love working here. She was angry with me for not obtaining a doctorate, which could permanently hurdle our progress. I did; I showed; returned satisfied next day on the same Taxi. She was the most significant reason motivating my Herculean effort! Love has some unexpected advantages, lateral. When it is damaged also exhibits some advantages, collateral. I experienced both!!!

Once there was a strike. The cooks and servers in the messes felt they are badly paid for their regular and timely services. Demanded increased salaries. Refused, they went on strike. They were out of bounds to Institute. They are all Pahadis of UP one of the poorest regions in the country. Only very few white collars used to see them or plead on their behalf. I was very active on their behalf along with some friends, like Pranab, Prafulla,

CKGK Pillai. By and large the authorities were hostile. So too the beneficiaries of these very docile and obedient workers. MLA Sumeer Singh came and tried. Mohan Poonamiya, the communist MP, mediated. A compromise was reached. All were happy. Messes were opened. Wages were slightly increased. But the workers are changed !

D B V Subrahmanyam and his poetry Recitals with Avakai and Pulihora are a great draw in those times. DBV was the son of the famous stage artist Shri DV Subbarao garu of Bandar. Because he was my room mate, the get together used to happen in my room. Research scholars used to be given bigger rooms and with attached Bath rooms. Pulihara was made in the room by any one or two. Avakai used to be contributed by me or Prof. KS Rao, reader in Chemical Engineering.

JOB HUNTING - TIFR, BARC, COLLEGES, UNIVERSITIES, SUBBARAO-CHEMISTRY, IISc.

I was the seniormost research scholar of BITS, Pilani in 1967. Two posts of Leturers were advertised in the department of Botany. I applied and very confident that I will get. By then I published 2 popular articles in science in the popular magazine, Caravan. Technical articles were 5 – Indian Forester, Cytologia, Chromosome Information Service, Science and Culture and Annals of Arid Zone. Interviews were held and I was not selected. Professor Muley, my godfather passed away. Prof. Pillai has gone to USA. Dr. MC Joshi was the head. He just took revenge, unusual for a teacher. In the beginning he was my favourite teacher due to his sweet talks. I joined him for the M.Sc dissertation work. It was on grasses. There I saw him manipulating experimental data of my seniors. My impression naturally fell. For Ph.D I left him as well as the subject of Ecology. His ambition was to become the first faculty to guide a Doctorate. This could not be achieved due to my volte face.

In hind sight, I think I would have got the job if only I visited his house for help, and or requested the director Lakshminarayanan, for help. His daughter was my student. And himself had a good impression of me. I did not do either of these and paid the heavy price. Only in 1973, I could get a University Lecturer Position that too in Odisha. What a price for not following the ways of the world.

Until then, I attended many interviews but rarely considered by Universities and colleges.The most memorable are the interviews for assistant posts at BARC, TIFR and IISc. The first was The Tata Institute of Fundamental Research. I was interviewed by a single man – a fair, lean, tall man with special looks in a room with a view of the sea and a beautiful painting on the wall. The building itself was very attractive; inside absolutely clean and good looking with Paintings on the wall at appropriate places, serenity ruling the place. Professor Obaid Siddique did not select me because I did not know mathematics and physics. Further more I had no interest in them. Dr. Siddique hails from an affluent family of Uttar Pradesh, a student of Aligarh, with socialistic views. His further studies were in England and became well known even for his doctoral studies. I have great liking for him.

The second interview was in Bhabha Atomic Research Centre. There were many candidates. Interview committee also was large. Several people asked us questions on many aspects of Cytogenetics of plants, animals, Humans and even Microbes. The Chairman was Dr. Gopal Ayengar. At the end he enquired about my doctoral thesis and the mechanism involved at BITS. He simply said you complete the present work and approach us.

Both of them were in 1966. After obtaining Ph.D in 1969, I attended another interview at Indian Institute of Science. I think there are only 4 candidates. But the committee had about 10 people. It was frightening. Almost half of them enquired of what I knew and did not. There was Seshachar, Gopal-Ayangar, Bachawat, Siddique, chaired by Satish Dhawan. After the interviews are over, I was called once again. Dr. Dhawan told we are seriously considering you. Lecturer post cannot be given to you, because you had no Post doctoral experience in the developed countries. Therefore, please meet the Head of Department tomorrow and discuss your future. Next day I met. The HOD curtly told that he is offering me a Senior Research Assistant post with 5 increments for a tenure of 5 years, the maximum possible. OR a Research Associate post with a fellowship of Rs 750 extendable annually. I "go as you advice" was my decision and opted for the former as it is financially more advantageous.

The galaxy of eminent scientists I faced here I never did again. In the department of Biochemistry, I began with good feelings from all circles.

Prof. Subba Rao, an emeritus Professor in the chemistry department evinced great interest in me and advised not to prefer small places, as they are big hells, but top Institutes such as Indian Institute of Science and not to compromise for small things. He came to BITS, where he knew me, from IISc, and returned.

Fig. 16: The Central Façade of BITS, Pilani, where the author obtained a Doctorate.

Fig. 17: Prof. B. N. Muley, head of Botany and the Benefactor and Guide of the Author.

Fig. 18: Group Photo of Author's Classmates, 1963-5, BITS, PILANI

Fig. 19: Authors's Teachers: *Prof. Pillai, Prof. Muley, Dr. Jain and Dr. Deshpande.*

Fig. 20: *Author receiving the degree of Ph.D from G.D. Birla, in 1969.*

Fig. 21: *Author with Dr. G. Subba Rao a batchmate and Friend.*

CHAPTER - 6

ERRANDS ALONG THE GANGA

DELHI
Tenneti and Nalini Mohan
'Chanchal Kapoor and Mendel Centenary

PRAYAGA, KASHI
Services Selection Board
Vedaraju, Sripada, Kasturi

JAIPUR
Hawa Mahal,
Amber Palace

MUZAFFARNAGAR
Celebrities
Two Notable Visits

DELHI, AGRA, LUCKNOW & ALIGARH
With Subba Rao

CALCUTTA
With Pranab Ray
Belur – Dakshineshwar,
Sibpur, Alipore
College Street, Rabindra Bharathi and Red Lights
Ashim Chatterjee

DELHI

New Delhi has a great role in my self improvement. During my education at Pilani, I had gone to Delhi and stayed at many places during 1961-1968. Initially I used to stay in the Hindu Mahasabha Bhavan – a kind of Choultry with free accommodation. Then I found on the same road, Birla Mandir, which has better facilities for travellers. They gave a preference to people from Pilani, the native place of the Birlas. For a few years, I continued to keep my small luggage in the cubicles they provide and sleep on floor, use common toilets and open bathing facilities. The entire day was used to be spent in Delhi University or Pusa Institute [IARI], most of the times. During such visits a research scholar from DU became friendly. May be because we speak the same language, Telugu. He was G. R. Rao working in Cytogenetics under Prof. S L Tandon. For some time I used to stay with him in Lodi Colony in a thatched tenement on the terraces of storied buildings called Barsati. I saw most of Delhi with him.

TENNETI AND NALINI MOHAN

Tenneti Viswanatham at Delhi, when he was an MP used to organise weekly meetings of mostly writers. Once I accompanied my cousin Mahidhara Nalini Mohan Rao, then Deputy Director of National Physical Laboratory. I thoroughly enjoyed that brief togetherness with Telugu and its practitioners. Many such incidents helped me never to part my roots.

Dr. Nalini was my cousin from maternal side. He was a Gold Medalist from Osmania University in Physics. His father, my uncle, Rama Mohan Rao was a famous Journalist, writer, a teacher of Marxism and a practical Communist. Nalini took his Doctorate from Moscow University in Tunnel Mechanics. He did not do well in science but excelled in its popularisation. Consequently, he was awarded the first National Award for Popularising Science. He is a great story teller appearing in every week in one or the other magazine in Telugu. He tried to join Pilani, but finally preferred New Delhi.

CHANCHAL KAPOOR AND MENDEL CENTENARY

Chanchal Kapoor was my senior and helped me with advice, information, suggestions and what not. It is she who took me to Dr. Swaminathan first and introduced other scientific personnel associated with him. Whenever in doubt, I always approached her as long as I was in Delhi. That is how I knew H K Jain, A T Natarajan, RP Sharma, R N Misra, B C Joshi, Pai, Mahinder Singh, Bansal. That is how I came to know of Mendel Centenary Symposium – a great event in Indian Science. This dealt with Cytology, Genetics and Plant Breeding *et al.* I attended this from inauguration to valedictory function. I covered most sessions to the extent possible. It was my desire to know as much and as many as possible. I did make some contacts and a few friends. This was in 1966. Very few conferences were organised and attended this well. India's top Scientists were here in cytogenetics and plant breeding. – Pal, Joshi, Ramanujam, Ramayya, Richaria, Janaki Ammal, Randhawa, Bor Thakur, to mention a few. From other countries, I remember Muntzing, Gustaffson, Singleton, Kihara, Chang, Borlaug, etc.

I learnt of Cannabis, Barley, Drosophila, Human Genetics, Dermatoglyphics, mammalian Genetics, here. Some practical methods also. It was a feast for me, a serious student of Science, but without any guidance and, direction, but groping. Experiences and Memories of this period helped me althrough my life, a life without any mentor, without friends, with suspicions and fears.

PRAYAGA, KASHI

After joining in M. Sc in Pilani, in July 1961, I applied for selection by the Services Selection Board [SSB]. I was called for an interview at Allahabad's Contonement. I was not selected but this is unique and unforgettable experience. We were 21 people, all from northern zone. All finished college obtaining a "c" certificate. I got a 'B' grade in it and running 19 yrs of age. It was for 3 days dealing with Hurdles, Field Crafts, Map Reading, General Knowledge, Public Speaking and Psychology. Only two were selected.

I concentrated on NCC for joining army, before I am 20, as an officer because of family's weak economic condition. I was the only one in my college who equitted well in studies as well as in NCC. But did not prepare well for the last hurdle and failed. I still have one more chance to try.

Afterwards I went to the local Engineering College, to meet my fellow villager and college mate, Vedaraju. I spent with him a few days in sight seeing. I saw Yamuna in the outskirts, before it becomes busy and Ananda Bhavan of Nehrus. He often used to loan me money, which I was always in dire need. He always kept this always confidential and remained a friend and admirer for long.

From here I went to Banares to meet my friends Sripada and Kasturi. The first was my senior in college now studying Mathematics at University. He was a Rashtriya Swayam Sevak, a Spartan in living and a communist in temperament and character. He showed me the important places. Unforgettable experiences. Kasturi was my classmate, now studying Masters in Botany.

Kashi was full of narrow lanes crowded by all types of Indians. Viswanath temple is unbelievably small and narrow, Ganga is crowded in its own way – Ghats, boats, people, floats of dirts and dead bodies. Each ghat is crowded by people and materials. But this mileu was considered sacred by Hindus from times immemorial. The celebrated philosophy of dirt must have emanated from here.

Sripada showed me the reason for all this. Adjascent to Viswanath Temple there is an enclosure with Gyan Vapi Mosque. At the back side of this structure is the interior of a temple. Yes. This is that reason. Our Viswanath temple is reduced to just accommodate an idol and a priest. Cannot these foreigners construct their

Mosque elsewhere instead of destroying our temple and building over it? Aurangzeb was supposed to have destroyed the original Vishwanath temple.

I lost touch of this great soul.

JAIPUR – HAWA MAHAL, AMBER PALACE

The first city I ever saw after Delhi was Jaipur. I saw an engineering marvel, the Hawa Mahal, in the heart of city, an eternally windy place in all its stories, and cool at that! It is just a thrill. I knew nothing else about this. Then I spent a day at Amber palace, with its ups and downs, camels and costumes, towards the periphery of the city. Wherever I went, pink was the dominant colour, giving an epithet to the city, Pink City.

MUZAFFARNAGAR

My leave vacancy employment ceases by the end of June 1968. Luckily I got a lecturership in the D A V College at Muzaffarnagar a few hours north to Delhi, on way to Dehradun. The stint here is memorable for many reasons. First is my continuous interaction with Douglas Dill from Canada who spend a few months here. Wherever may be his other works, I remember making a model of DNA along with him. It was as if Watson and Crick were making it in 1953. Excitable effort.

While many remarkable events were taking place at Pilani, I was employed as a lecturer in Botany by D A V College, Muzaffar Nagar, a district town 300 miles North East of Delhi. I joined in this job, in July 1968.

I did the writing of my thesis here. The principal Dr. Agarwal, Botany Professor, Dr. Kaushik, gave me every possible help and fulfilled every need of mine during those hectic days. Another great help was Mr. Yashvir Singh Gujjar, the leader of Students and Shri K V Shastri, a lecturer in Zoology. In fact, every one connected to me was generous. They were very memorable days indeed! Anil Kumar Tyagi was my student at that time, rose to great heights in science, Yash Vir preferred to be in UP Politics. Several occupied very high positions. For many years this place continued to be in my life.

BAJPAYEE, CHANDRASEKHAR, TARAKESWARI SINHA

In this college there is a tradition to invite some socially and / or politically important personalities to address the students on some occasion. Thus, I had an opportunity to see Chandrasekhar from Balia and Tarakeswari Sinha from Bihar from very close quarters and hear them and observe their mannerisms and body languages. I was proudly shown to visiting dignitaries, as a Madrasi show piece of India. I also met Atal Behari Bajpayee on another occassion. The teachers are on strike – hunger strike. On one particular day, it was my turn to sit. Atalji and his entourage visited our tent and talked to all. To me he asked whether I am comfortable in a new land and assured that soon I will adjust with others and others with me. This was memorable. Tarakeswari was very Charming and a forceful speaker.

TWO NOTABLE VISITS

A notable event of those days was my visit to Deoband's Islamic University. This was possible due to a student of mine – Shahid Ahmad Siddique. Incidentally he was my first student who did a project on Grasses of Muzaffarnagar. Our association was good. The second visit was to a Farm of a close relative and Political Associate of Shri Chaudhary Charan Singh. On a Sunday his grand nephew came to my residence on a Tractor and simply 'ordered' me to get in. Then he drove to his Farm some 15 miles away. The entire family greeted me, gave a very good lunch with Jat delicacies. The boy brought me back to my residence. He was my student and was very happy with my working like most students. Incidentally this is the same family Dr. Chenna Reddy paid a visit with his baton and lunched, when he was the Governor of Uttar Pradesh!

Another continuous association was with the family of K V Sastry, a lecturer in Zoology simultaneously working for his doctorate. A self confident and courageous soul, a very co-operative wife and a very sweet daughter Yamini. I missed them a lot in my whole life when I left Muzaffarnagar towards the end of 1969.

Then there was my foremost friend, student-like, Yashvir Singh Gujjar, who passed M.Sc in Botany, a student leader, and associated with me as an apprentice on the advice of the principal and Professor of Botany. He was a constant companion helping on every matter, doing things as per my instructions and helping me on anything possible. We never misused each other. We appreciated each other and Teachers were very happy for the changes in him he always addressed me as "Guruji". His doctoral guide was surprised at this basic respect towards me and said so. Prof. A.B. Gupta of Meerut University changed his conduct towards me ever after. He gradually dropped the caste suffices and remained just a Yash Vir.

SHAHID AHMAD SIDDIQUI and DEOBAND

Siddique was my student in M. Sc Botany during 1968-70. In his 2nd year he was allotted to me to do his research project. I asked him to survey various places in and around Muzaffarnagar and Deoband, his native place for grasses. He was doing enthusiastically whatever we both discussed and decided. He was so happy that he invited me to Deoband. He gave a good briefing of the place especially of its Islamic University, about which I never heard of, until then. We roamed about the place, the mix of Hindu and Muslim cultures and lives. He took me to the Seminary - University. Strict discipline everywhere in all respects; most people are fair and meticulously dressed in purest white. We sat with one smiling faculty whom Siddique knows. We shared tea, some snacks and talked things at random. He was very knowledgeable. Just before parting, he enquired of my native place and asked about my caste, he exclaimed, Oh! It is you people who prevented the spread of Islam in this country. Islam conquered nearly half of India, we should have taken over fully but for your caste's control of Hinduism – pat came the reply. With smiling countenances we parted. But I learnt a historic truth.

DELHI, AGRA, LUCKNOW, ALIGARH

In research, often we get tired, bored, exasperated and what not. On one such situation me and my friend Subbarao a research scholar in zoology thought of an outing to refresh our spirits. The result was a passage to Delhi first, limited to the Indian Agricultural Research Institute. It was in the news for the suicides of two scientists: Dr. Joseph and Dr. Shah. Also a magazine was coming from there concentrating on the problems of scientific workers. First we met the editor of this magazine, Dr. Abrol in soil physics, so as to develop an insight into the problems he faces in dealing with our welfare. Then we spent some time in Agronomy with Prof. Singh whose colleague Prof. Shah committed suicide not long ago. Unfortunately, Prof. Singh died of rabies sometimes later from his own pet dog! The third person we met was Prof. Ramdas Menon, the oldest and most illustrious of the three. It is in his lab that his assistant Dr. Joseph had to commit suicide against injustice. Prof. Menon told us about Joseph tragedy, how he was sought to be implicated and the role of M S Swaminathan in his rescue. He also narrated how some major scientists are trying to improve ICAR through Justice Gajendra Gadkar Commission. He also told us about JBS Haldane, who just passed away and how the Dasavatharas of Mythology are suggestive of the evolutionary concept.

Then we moved to Agra to meet Prof. Sinha of Botany in Agra College. Some time ago this department was very famous for the researches of K C Mehta on the rusts of wheat, a type of fungi. We became tourists to see Fatehpur Sikri and Tajmahal, especially the Yamuna hinterland.

We moved to Aligarh Muslim University to meet Dr. K S Rai, who became famous for controlling some insect pests through their genetics. We enjoyed talking with him. The last man we met was Prof Chaudhary of Botany, who lamented the eroding of values in life and professions. Of course we found him frustrated because of his field, Anatomy, by then lost its importance. A regal person full of affection and charm towards youth.

We moved to Lucknow to meet the world famous sociologist, Prof. Radhakamal Mukerjee, the then Vice Chancellor and brother of the historian, Radha Kumud Mukerjee. Unfortunately we could not. Fatigue sets in. Therefore we spent some time on Gomati river and visited some historical places such as Imambara, etc. Incidentally this is the place of a student of our department, I used to be fond of, Asha Lata Sang.- quite an interesting name and person.

CALCUTTA WITH PRANAB RAY

By chance, I happened to get friendly with a classmate of Prafulla Chandra, my friend from Pharmacy. He is Pranab Ray. We used to discuss all matters under the sky, from Literature to Politics and Science in between. He is from Calcutta close to Utpal Dutt, son of a Railway officer and a nephew of Prof. Chaudhary the Head of Electronics at BITS. Eversince, I changed my route of going home. I always took the Toofan Express from Delhi to reach Calcutta, spend a few days with Pranab and move to Andhra preferably by Janata Express. In many such escapades, me and Pranab saw a good deal of Calcutta staying in his house at Liluah's Railway Quarters.

BELUR, SIBPUR, ALIPORE

We went to Ramakrishna Mission at Belur. We visited the Kali temple called Dakshineswar, built by Rani Rashmoni during the domination of East India Company. For some time we sat on the steps leading to Ganga with our feet in the waters. We talked with many people there. We found peace despite all those busy times and large number of people and visitors.

On the other side of the Ganga is Sibpur. It is famous for a Banyan Tree whose main trunk is not known. It is in the middle of a garden christened as National Botanical Garden. In a corner of this garden was a building housing the offices of Indian Botanical Survey. It dates back to East India Company. Many famous scientists work in these buildings. Large number of rare plants are maintained in these NBG. Some plants which could not be brought were maintained here as specimens of herbarium.

Pranab took me to Alipore Central Jail. This was famous for keeping and trying Aurobindo Ghosh. We wanted to see their cells and other places associated with them. Alas! We were not given permission even for a stroll inside!

COLLEGE STREET

For all young people the college street is the most important, teaming with students, stationary shops, book stalls, tea stalls, Second-hand book shops, noises – all on the left side. On the right, are the colleges, and hostels of men and women. There is always some activity. In some tea stall some students are debating some issue all the time. The day I went there women students were agitating for some thing. Most groups were leftists.

Some kilometers from here is the house of Rabindranath Tagore. It was converted into a University for solely arts called as Rabindra Bharathi. We were walking towards it. Suddenly came to our sight scenes I never saw before, nor saw in a cinema nor heard of. They are the multistored buildings lined by females and their dresses put for drying, and the women standing as if in rows gesticulating to passers by on the street below. Very strange spectacle. Pranab told me they are prostitute dens, those living there will have no deliverance. This is also our India. I saw this some where around 1965-66. I have not forgotten it to this day – human misery is such.

NABADWEEP : Krishna Consciousness

Once we travelled to Nabadweep in the far south of Calcutta. Pranab told me that Geeta Govindam was written here. Yes I told him that my mother used to sing Jayadeva's Ashta Padis and teach them to others and I used to write them for them. He showed me an old temple where these were written originally by Jayadeva. The Consciousness of Srikrishna originated here and showed me the temple of Krishna consciousness in white marble.

ASHIM CHATTERJEE AND HIS ADMIRERS

One evening several of us met on the outside of a building in Liluah which is vacant. So many questions and doubts to be answered by me, because they all believed that I am the most educated and knowledgeable. A man slight in built asked towards the end how can we hit the peoples' enemies and yet survive. For this, we need good shelters not easily accessible to our enemies. Examples? Then I drew the map of Eastern Ghats. One has to come down the slopes of Eastern Ghats and go back the slopes after the work. We should also be able to travel on the top of slope all along from north to south. Theoretically, from somewhere from the south of Eastern Ghats in Andhra one can go upto Siliguri unsuspected and thence to Himalayan foothills and Himalayas. This is the importance of Hills and Forests and local people. All heard me seriously. The daper man complemented me saying we have a theoretician without jargons and shook hands, collected his small bag and walked away. He just went under ground - Pranab told me that he was Ashim Chatterjee, a gold medalist of Calcutta University in Physics Masters and also Chemistry Masters. He was to become a very significant leader in the communist revolutionary movement of Bengal in the years to come, believing in revolutions within revolutions, as a periodical resurrection or rejuvenation.

CHAPTER - 7

BACK TO ROOTS

A Munikhanda
Literary and culture personalities
Ideal Family

Caste high Class low
Quest for Education

Political Consciousness
Social Reformers and Communists
Most tragic character in a Disciplined family
Jealousies and Consequences
Vedavati and Leela, Austian Characters
Some Uniquenesses

A MUNIKHANDA

This village used to be inhabited by Veginati sect of Brahmins. I believe, after observing them for years sporadically, that most sects are just one, differentiated only by regions where they settled and some customs they adopted from the region. Thus, Veginatlu of Vegi, Velanatlus of Velanadu, Kasannatlu of Kosalanadu, Telaganyulu of Telangana, Mulakanatlu of Mulakanadu, are all but one. I further believe that it is from them some were drafted to work or drifted towards the rulers from their vedic dharma and karmas. They became the Niyogis. Since administration demands tact, wisdom and the like they gradually distinguished themselves. The others were the migrants from south the Dravillu and Srivaishnavulu. All these people maintain, foolishly their individualities even after announcing their adherence to vedic dharma and karmas ! Madhwas are another variety. If searched there may be some others!

Veginatis were widely scattered as some people say due to their various desires and foolishness. Thus clusters of these are present at Parlakemidi in Odisha, Vijayanagaram, Kotipalli, Polavaram Island, Krapa, Porur, Tenkasi, etc. But the highest concentration has been in the village of, currently known as, Munganda, considered as the capital of Veginatis. In fact when ever an eccentric or stupid or unsuccessful Brahmin is encountered, he is suspected to belong to this sect!

Every summer I shall be there. My mother's two elder sisters live there and so most of our clan - about 300 houses arranged in a typically French mode - one long street with laterals branching out at regular intervals. A canal goes around it on one side, supplying water to the tank - a famous one in the region!

Munganda is a village with a hoary past in between Amalapuram and Gannavaram in the Delta area of East Godavari district - the latter is the place of Aqueduct over a tributary of Godavari, Vainatheyam. From Rajahmundry, take a bus to Razole to get down at Munganda. Ask anyone 60+ about this village. The story is something you may savour, but in disbelief.

There was a small building with a long table and chairs and many almirahs of books all along the walls. It is surrounded by a ground with a Badminton Court and a well with the surrounding floor cemented. This is popularly known as Bhavanam – A Trade Mark, a kind of Brand for this village, a uniqueness. This houses the AIR. By evening people gather to listen to Radio Programmes especially the news. Quite until late they sit around Bhavanam and discuss the news of the world, the country and the state as if they are involved! Though an occasional visitor to this village, I had the singular fortune of using this library to read books!

Veyipadagalu [Thousand Hoods] of Viswanatha Satyanarayana is one such. The author won the prestigious Jnanapeetha Award in later years. On hearing about this from my Telugu teacher, I wanted to read and expressed my desire to many. But in vain. When in Munganda once, I told the same to my uncle, husband of my mother's sister. He went to Bhavanam and brought home; put conditions about its usage. The book is one of the biggest in Telugu, consisting of over a Thousand pages. I used to go to his house every morning, sit cross-legged with the book on the Vyasapeetham, a book-holding device. It took nearly 10 days to read it. I forgot most of it, but not Dharma Rao and Ganachari.

Another was Kokkoka Sastram, a treatise on romance and sex. My cousin, Mohan Rao brought it secretly. We both went to the cocoanut groves; sat in a secluded place and opened the pages. We understood nothing. The vocabulary was unintelligible. It did not interest us. Probably we are not ready for it. But an experience nevertheless.

The latest best book was "Kollayi Kattitenemi" meaning what if only a small cloth is worn" alluding to Mahatma Gandhi's minimal attire, deeds must be great. This won a Sahitya Academy Award. The author was Mahidhara Rama Mohana Rao, my uncle.

ROW OF SEVEN BANYAN TREES-A HERITAGE SITE

The village has a Brand. The seven Banyan trees – lining in a row, by the side of the road leading to Gannavaram on the Vainatheyam. Legends tell that the Seven Maharishis sat under these seven trees and performed their Tapasysas. Therefore, the Agraharam was then a Munikhanda, gradually transforming into the present Munganda. The Banyans have gone; So is the tradition of scholarship!

THE VILLAGE TANK - ANOTHER HERITAGE SITE

Yet another Brand is the village tank that gets periodical water from the Godavari. It is never cleaned. It is never polluted. It is used only for drinking and the purposes of temples. Weeds were rarely removed. If removed the boys from the agraharam only will do. Fish are not allowed to be extracted by any one - If some tried to catch them clandestinely, it would be a mis-adventure. I am aware of some murders too. But once in two years the local people are allowed to capture most of them and not all. They are not auctioned for revenue. The tank water is reputed to be the main reason for the intelligence, sometimes excessive, of the village youth. Most of them learn swimming in this tank and breath control in this water. The entire village exhibits a stake in these three brands. All these are under the control of the Panchayat for which, a traditional Brahmin has been a President for more than a decade that I knew. He was a Communist. This is perhaps another specialty of this village for the whole Konaseema, nay for the entire district. May be in the entire state.

LITERARY AND CULTURE PERSONALITIES

The village had many Sanskrit scholars like Khandavilli Suryanarayana Sastry and Pulle Umamaheswara Sastry. The latter was much revered by the Sankaracharya and was decorated by the President of India. Mahidhara Ramamohana Rao, famous as a teacher of Communism in Andhra, was a Sahitya Academy awardee for his political and period novel "Kollayi Kattitenemi" [what if a loin cloth only is worn] hailed from here. His father Suryanarayana was the founder of Brahma Samajam in Andhra following Raja Rammohan Roy. His son Dr. Nalini Mohan Rao was the first recipient of the Indira Gandhi Award for Science Popularisation. The village produced many Scientists, Professors, Musicians and Poets. Ajanta and Ellora two poets of different genres also come from this village - The former won National and the latter state level Sahitya Academy Awards.

PANDITA JAGANNATHA RAYALU OF MOGHUL COURT

The most notable was Upadrashta Jagannatha Pandita Rayalu who adorned the court of Shajahan, loved and married a Muslim courtier Lavangi! Pandita Rayalu has written Alla Upanishat - cream of Islam in Sanskrit - and Asif Puranam after the noble uncle of Shajahan who helped him against the conspirators. These are not well known unfortunately. However, it is not certain whether Rayalu has really belonged to this place as strongly claimed by the villagers even now.

SARASWATULA RAMAYANAM BY RAMASASTRY

It was believed that Ramayanam written by a person by name Saraswatula Rama Sastry is one of the many versions of Ramayanam available on record. It is baffling that people of this clan themselves do not know this. It is believed that his clan is one of the six families which migrated from Vijayanagaram to the northern Island of Konaseema, in search of greener pastures!

It is surprising that the descendents of both the above greatmen, belonging to Upadrashta and Sarawatula made no efforts to do any research work into their ancestors. It is interesting to note that both these claim ancestry to the Sage Koundinya! Politically conscious, steeped in tradition, knowledge and vibrant, not a dull day in this place - with temple functions, marriages, feasts, cultural meets, special musical intonation of the other wise witty conversations and above all an affinity to the ethereal tank.

MY GRAND FATHER'S LIBRARY FOR CHILDREN

After retirement at the age of 58, my grand father collected his Provident Fund. He did not give it to any one including his wife. Did not buy some gold. He simply bought children's books – such as Bharatam, Ramayanam, Panchatantram in Pictures and came to the village he decided to settle – Munganda Agrahaaram. Every one was laughing at him for his foolishness. His wife was abusing him. For several days he became a butt of ridicule. But I became an admirer of him; saw the books; perused most of them getting clearances from him. Because at that time we were also in that village, temporarily.

CADAVER SERVICE BY MY GRAND FATHER

No work. No income. When some one died, there was an abnormal delay in carrying the cadaver for cremation, for more than one reason. Then he offered himself to be one of the Four Pal -Bearers! Every one welcomed. Because the distance involved in the carriage is long. It did not occur to any one that he is a senior citizen! Soon he became a regular pal-bearer for who ever dies. Later some people gave him some money too. A man who participated in Freedom Movement, regularly helped people with cash and kind had to become an honorary staff member of the Department of Undertakers!

DISCIPLINE AND STABILITY

I saw so many old rich families gradually degenerating under economic and social pressures, except a few. The most significant one is the Khandavilii family of Munganda due to values and discipline.

My own grand father, Sitaramayya, a highly educated landlord descended to poverty and silently use to weep in the grove behind Mamidisetty's house, in Munganda. On the other hand my grand mother, Ramanamma, steered her family of 5 from sheer poverty to prosperity, only due to planning and discipline. No rich family treated me well or properly, although I am good in education continuously from childhood. Wealth alone matters, not education as Brahmins claim. Further I am considered a fool, just as my father and grand father; Heritage! Such mind sets are bred by Agrahaarams.

It is a memorable sight. We used to form a large column of students who would pedal about 10 miles to the nearest college at Amalapuram excitedly and return equally excitedly in the evening - day after day, week after week, month after month and year after year.

POLITICAL CONSCIOUSNESS

The village or Agraharam has been famous for long and for a variety of reasons. During our childhood we never understood why the people used to fiercely fight with each other. As we grew up to go to college we realised.

There were Traditionalists, Patelites, Nehruites, Socialists and Communists. All gather in the evening at "Bhavanam" the Panchayat office, to listen to regional, national and international news. Discussions flare up and ultimately end up in the "Noothi Pallem" - the cemented circular platform around the well situated on one side of the Bhavanam. For the onlooker it was a very well informed, exciting, provocative and unforgettable pastime for 3-4 hours.

From Lenin to Krushchev and Mao, Churchill, de Gaulle and Adenauer, Nehru, Patel, Bose, Jayaprakash Narain, Lohia, Krishna Menon, Prakasam, Rajaji and Kala Venkata Rao become neighbours, friends, and foes in turns.

Occasionally, Geddam Kesava Rao comes to chide all of them to tell Nehru - our man, united Sukarno, NKrumah, Nasser and Tito and won Chou-en-lai to confront imperialism, exactly like Gandhi would have liked. This tall man, who did an MA from jail sold all his land for the Freedom Movement, wrote a treatise on

"How to revitalize Congress" served as Political Secretary to Andhra Kesari T. Prakasam, the then CM and finally died unsung leaving his wife a destitute.

Many went to jail either in the freedom movement or as communist revolutionaries as in no other village.

SOCIAL REFORMERS AND COMMUNISTS

In the early Fifty's Mahidhara Suryanarayana from the village married his daughter to a Kamma caste lawyer on principles of communism and arranged their stay in his house in the agraharam for the carriage of post-marital customs. His two sons, the Munganda Brothers, became, subsequently famous communists of Andhra Pradesh and teachers of this philosophy to the cadres.

Also a child widow, by name Somidevamma, was educated by her father against the then prevailing traditions who rose to become a Professor of Chemistry subsequently in Andhra University.

When the Malabar Special Police took the communist Dr. Saraswatula Suryanarayana for killing during early 1950s to an island in the nearby Godavari, the peasantry got him released. This doctor is a permanent president of all communist meetings in that region. He will become very emotional within a minute or two, loose his lung power and sits down within five minutes. This is both a matter of fun as well as great veneration. His home harboured several fugitive communists during 1950s, who ate off his wife, my aunt.

Venkata Reddy ran away from Army with his rifle and tried to give training to revolutionaries [he was caught at Ryali and shot dead in Public view in front of the famous temple there]. The great Mamidisetty brothers - Chandranna, Veeranna, Sooranna - communists helping anyone in need.

For long the Panchayat president was a communist Brahmin, who used to say brahmin has to be a communist as per shastras! Prof. Kosambi maintained this view all life. So too many leftist brahmins, such as U.R. Ananta Murty.

PILFERING BOOKS

My grand father was studying at Rajahmundry and had plans to do law to become a pleader in the footsteps of many national leaders in those days. Therefore, he was slowly preparing the furniture, buying books, and the like. In those days he had a palatial house at Vakatippa in front of his Cocoanut Grove. His decadence started and grew in the form of 3 women! His mother, his wife and his sister. And he is not worldly wise! He lost his bungalow to the chicanery of Geddam Sarveswara Rao. Most property was dissolved due to the excessive and irresponsible affections of his mother towards her daughter's family of a dozen people, half of which prey on him for 3 summer months every year and for a dozen years. His wife never allowed him to study! Consequently, he lost the Bungalow, the furnitures, the books and finally the cocoanut grove! Who ever could lay his hands on his books, the books obliged to go with the new master. At last, only 2 books – Geetanjali of Tagore and a Botany Text remained with us.

When I was in Pilani, for nearly 7 years, I used to send books to my family at Munganda. My brother used to show them to others. One used to take them never to return. This gentleman was Pinninti Ramam, a very popular figure with this wily habit.

Not knowing, I continued to send home, now in Hyderabad, where my books were freely given to others with a comment "He left us on the roads; looked after his own interests; why look after his books ?" The biggest beneficiary of this largesse was G R K Sastry of Munganda and a relative. When I asked him to tell what books did he take - the phone always went dead.

Many of my books were stolen from my house, predictably by student visitors. Some faculty like Sambandham take books but never return. Faculty stealing books from the library of the University is another story!

MARRIAGE PROPOSALS BLOCKED

Marriage proposals blocked for selfish reasons by the family ruled by Ridge-Gourd Syndrome. In this family if a boy is borne all concentration is on education, fine. But keeping his marriage in mind and the girl in mind, not the merits of the boy or any special qualities possessed. So focus is on a quick job and earnings and settling with a woman, sooner than necessary! If a girl is borne, the focus is on a marriage; all else guided towards this. Thus, I and my family were fully controlled – our residence, our education, our jobs, our families, our works, our thoughts and generate a determination to continue this policy. There were thus attempts to interfere with me many times. First they wanted me to go for typing and shorthand to be eligible for a clerk post in the government by the age of 18! Then they desired me to become a teacher after graduation to remain local. After Masters, they wanted that I become a Lecturer in a College. My desire was first to become an Army Officer, failing which a University Lecturer for which I must achieve a Doctorate. When I succeeded in this, they selected my bride, whom I never knew, met or even saw to keep control on me. But other offers were coming. They blocked all of them I never knew of them. Some info was revealed after a decade or so! Because I did not oblige them, they ostracized me! I knew of three marriage proposals, far better atleast overtly. They changed the residences of my family 3 times, but the increased expenditure and other responsibilities are mine. The point here is, decisions will be theirs, but costs and consequences have to be borne by me. These so called communists did not know either Engel's Family or the Booklet "How to be a good Communist" written by Trotsky or improved by Li Shao Chi. Simply a kind of Patriarchal Tyranny through superior economic condition and there from social dominance. A better human becomes a victim!

JEALOUSIES AND CONSEQUENCES

Just as prostitution was the most ancient profession, jealousies are the most basic and universal among humans. Interestingly even the so-called learned people, Brahmins are no exception. In fact, they are more prone to this, especially regarding education. Two examples, Durgayya Sastry's grand son Babi gradually ascended the ladder of education to the pinnacle, a doctorate. Many did not like – both relatives and others. The grand father was accused of swindling the funds of the Co-operative Bank and was sought to be punished by the Kapus of Tillakuppa Village. In my case, it was worse. The Weavers' society of Jaggannapeta, accused my father of educating his son, me, to levels unheard of in those places, a doctorate, with their funds. They harassed him so much that he succumbed to his ailments. The Registrar of Co-operative Societies was convinced by me, alas, after my father passed away, that their allegations and activities are inhuman besides being wrong.

SUICIDE ATTEMPT BY VYASU, MY BROTHER

After my father's death in December, 1964, my family moved to Munganda and staying although in a dilapidated house, just because it is two houses away from our uncle, Dr. Suryanarayana's house. There is a camaraderie between my brothers – Vyasu and Sattee on one hand and Suryam and Raghupathi, the last two children of my uncle, on the other. During 1965 summer, the family of Pushpavathi, the eldest daughter of my uncle came to spend vacation. She has 5 daughters, Suryakumari being the eldest.

Suryam and Raghu started teasing Vyasu that Kumari is in love with him and goaded him to draw her figures and then write love letters next. This fun and frolic continued for some time, Suryam-Raghu acting as intermediaries. While the prank continued for some time, a love letter fell into the hands of her father and our uncle. Whether it is by chance or by design is not known to me.

My uncle came to my house angrily and beat Vyasu while taking food. As if insufficient, Bhaskaram the father of Kumari, came angrily again and caught hold of Vyasu's hair, and began beating, shouting invectives, both non-stop. During the next few days the episode snow balled as a juicy scandal and all were making fun of Vyasu. Unable to absorb, he tried to commit suicide by consuming some pesticide. Fortunately it was very dilute he could be saved by the efforts of my mother, and two grand mothers- Sundaramma and Pullamma.

Two questions arise here. When it is a mere prank among friends, why it is made into an issue? How and why the two Pranksters were not pulled up for this dangerous game? When my uncle's daughter, Roja, received a love letter, how did he deal with it - in gross deviation with the present one? The most ridiculous aspect is that this girl, Kumari was offered in marriage to me a few months later when I visited them at Kakinada, unaware of this whole story? Just because of our bad times, they can give us a penny of help and derive pounds of advantages? The entire clan was doing this on all of us for years! A kind of filial imperialism.

MOHANRAO

My closest friend in those times was my cousin Mohanrao, son of my mother's sister. He was from Munganda, famous for his short cycle and eating homeo pills, a left hander and sharp shooter, has great reflexes and shrewd mind and very hard working. He was always my leader. I was suffering from dysentery once for a spell of 10 days. We then went to my place Jaggannapeta, and asked my mother to prepare Idly and Cocoanut Chutney to eat! The dysentery disappeared. What a hilarious time was that. When we develop a desire to see a cinema, we together visit on cycle my grand father's place whether it is nearby Narendrapuram or far away Ryali. Sentiments will produce Rs 5. Sometimes we used see 3 cinemas one after another. He would balance the cycle, but pedaling used to be done by me sitting behind. As I did not know cycling. There were many stories on our escapades. This includes his secret marriage with a girl in the neighbourhood in the local temple! Of course, this turned out to be a childhood tantrum-cum-craze!

We never used to like others to interfere with us. Once we went to Nedunuru. Our cousin was following. We did not like and told him so. He continued. I just bent him and he gave a few blows on his back. He stopped coming with us. He was our great friend.

I got him an impossible seat at BITS, illegally, which was responsible for his subsequent affluence. He selected my lady love and arranged our meetings. I did not make his marriage, as accused. But he was responsible for my unpopularity among the relations. When he was dying no one cared to inform me, the closest of his friends. Entire clan behaved like a gang a few decades later and justified too. No wonder communism failed in India, so miserably.

BABURAO

Babu Rao is a paternal Cousin of Mohan Rao, living in the same house; therefore my friend too. He was senior to me by an year, in the college. He was also my colleague in NCC. But he did not shine well. He is a good man unaware of wiles of society. He was neglected by father. Mother did not care; she was more in league with her daughter in all their activities, good, bad and ugly. He did not have any sincere friends, except Ramarao, Chekuri. We never differed seriously and he was always nice with me. Once both of us went to Kakinada to the Battalion Hq on his Moped. Completing the work, we were returning the next day. I just requested him to allow me to drive after Draksharama. He gave. Normally he never gives. We were traveling towards Kotipalli. Suddenly a few cows came running on the road. Instead of using the Brake I increased the accelerator. Collision with a cow was the result. Pedal broke. We both rolled towards the road side storm drain. Baburao did not loose his temper. He stood smiling. From then onwards he drove with great difficulty until Amalapuram, where it was repaired. He was a silent admirer. He failed in B.Sc. I wanted to take him next year to Pilani for higher studies as it happened with Mohan Rao and Prasadam. He did not have initiative or dash. He obeyed the parents and married; a good marriage. Thus, ended our association of 4 years! An unfortunate soul.

VEDAVATI AND LEELA, Austian Characters

They came on a courtesy visit, on their way back to

Hyderabad, the place of their work and living. Seeing my mother sad, they pressed to know the reason. After knowing, they gave Rs 3000, to cover the expenditure for my two years in college. And never asked for its return, but given back after a few years. These two women are cousins of my mother as well as my father. They are good and humane, and great singers. They are abandoned by 5 brothers for very unhealthy reasons accepted by a majority. They were ostracized left to fend for themselves. I am the second to be ostracized for different unreasons, cruelty being common. We signify the culture of our clan and its overt and covert characteristics.

My family's guide and philosopher advised my brothers to fleece me in as many ways as possible for, I am supposed to have a lot of money. Therefore we cheat you – said Vyasu the elder of the duo of my younger brothers, in front of our mother. I do not know how far this goading was true. But they did indulge in benefiting secretly through cheating me but injuring and insulting openly and getting filial applause for these actions.

COMMERCE IN EDUCATION AND LIFE

Surya Bhaskara Sarma, later it was known, was financed by his future father-in-law to do masters on the condition of marrying his daughter. Life became successful by this deal. Education also is commerce. To be frank I also hoped some one would come for me too, but none came. When came at last, it was after the masters while doing a Doctorate; it was for maintaining family. Too late. I was offered 4 acres of prime delta land, if I marry a Karnam's niece who may be only a matriculate. Family is interested in the land for its revenue, getting which is the duty of the eldest son towards his siblings.

DISAPPEARANCE OF KSB SARMA IN DELHI

K S B SARMA, a good friend of mine was reported missing. After some years I was told that it is the misbehaviour and a probable infidelity of wife that made him runaway. So the blame was put on her, without trying to trace him or pursuing through the police. This is typical Munganda! I thought of this seriously analyzing from all sides. I developed the following story as the most plausible explanation for his disappearance. It is as follows:

He always uses cycle for all his works and drives it fast. In one of his such journeys he must have met an accident, injured and died. No identities. Inquiries may not have been done properly. All these are possibilities, for, today's communication technologies were non-existent then. This is a realistic thesis on his fate knowing his psyche, habits and Delhi. His cousin, Prasadam never thought it fit to inform me !

SOME UNIQUENESSES

Literacy was always high, especially of women due to a middle school. It was a mystery why this was closed, when newer schools were being opened. Strangely further a politically and culturally conscious village just kept quiet!

People are very ecological at times when this word was not known. The tank is well maintained with adequate plants for waste removal and fish were not allowed to be caught at will. Entry points were regulated !

Munganda perhaps is the only village in Konaseema that can boast of a Ayurvedic, a Homeo and an Allopathic Doctor, and all in the same street, Red Cross street!

People here are very violent, if necessary. Many were farmers and landlords. They maintained weapons, first rifles and later spears. Murders did happen in some families, but remained clandestine.

When fish eaters invaded the tank for catching the fish, the village youth defended it with the weapons. In that scuffle, a Brahmin youth killed two of them, preventing the mobs from advancing. He was nick-named Tiger for his valor, a communist and became a journalist.

This was the only village having a Brahmin as the Panchayat President, successively. He was a Communist. Brahmins here are famous for amorous activities – extra-marital relations, out-station Devadasi relationships, sexual relations with working class in the groves.

There was a happy-go-lucky man, my roommate for some time while in college at Amalapuram, Kishtappa Khandavilli, a memorable fellow, full of mirth. Whoever knows him even for a brief time will never forget him for a very rare quality – not just generosity but for his calligraphy. There was none else in S K B R College in those 4 years I studied, in this craft.

Male cooks of Munganda were very famous for long. They used to be hired for all major functions - small and big, in the district. Some of them even opened hotels even before independence. Their descendents ran afternoon and evening shops with a varieties of dry eateries until mid-60s.

This village has a habit of undoing their own people with talents, merits and services. Godavarti Bhaskara Rao' Labours– Motivating children to sing revolutionary songs, collecting Folk songs associated with various occasions in society were never appreciated. While they boast of Jagannatha Pandita Rayalu of Shajahan's Court as their native, they are not aware of Saraswatula Ramayanam of Ramasastry. They do not wish to claim their own – Father-son-nephew-literary figures. A very self-defeating people, noted for cynicism, sarcasm and such talents!

No wonder that a famous place for curing mental illnesses is in a neighbouring village, Chiratapudi and the book – "The last Brahmin" has come from this soil suggesting that greatness of Brahmins, whatever it was, has come to an end; so their value. Otherwise how can one explain a thoroughfare to Isakapudi through the middle of the village, when there is a vast space all around ?

When a boy is born the family begins to think how soon to make him an earner and when a girl is born, how soon to marry her off. A Veginati psyche.

Yet the village is famous for Vedic knowledge and heritage standing among the most illustrious among Telugu people.

SPIRIT: THEN AND NOW

Seshamma, the brahmin donated 50 sovereigns of gold and worked in the rice fields and participated in protests to show solidarity with working class. This is the human spirit in those times here. Now it is replaced by jealousies, ingratitudes and chicaneries of Mohan Raos, Sattulus aka Satyanarayana and their brothers and sisters, multiplying.

EPILOGUE: A small village of 300 houses with such a glorious past - today is a mere shadow with no Memorabilia for the posterity to derive either satisfaction or inspiration, not even a common room, despite wallowing in the yankee culture of money!

Fig. 22: *My Mother and my Siblings, 2 Brothers and 2 Sisters.*

Fig. 23: *My Grand Mother [Step-Mother of my Father] her three daughters and two Sons.*

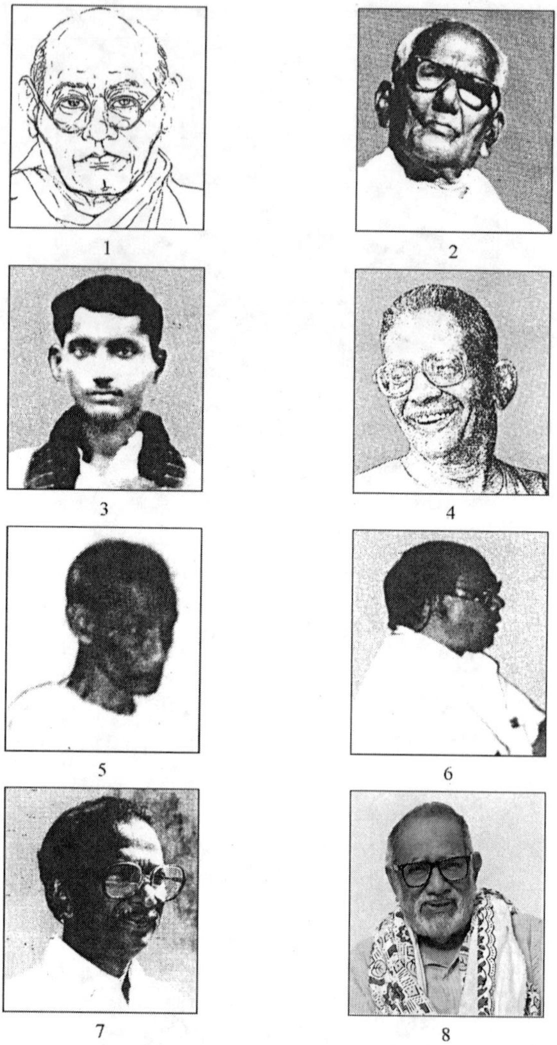

Fig. 24: Eight significant people in my Family :

1. Gopalakrishnayya, Maternal Grand father, 2. Sitaramayya, Paternal Grand Father, 3. Ramachandra Rao. Father, 4. Ram Mohan Rao, Maternal Uncle, 5. Suryanarayana, Paternal Uncle, 6. Satya Murty, Maternal Uncle, 7. Viswanatham [Ajanta] and 8. Sitarama Shastri, Maternal Cousins

CHAPTER - 8

HOBBYING WITH EMOTIONS

The angel that presided over my birth Said

"Little Creature,
formed of joy and mirth,
Go, work and love
Without the help
of anything on earth"

Blake

A time has come all of a sudden, when the mind and heart became full of feelings, thoughts, doubts, questions, fears, hopes and unable to express. Then why not resort to paper and pencil to keep on jotting them; gradually emerging into patterns, a poetry. From 1966 they must be about 60. This has become a medium of expression. Some 40 remained, rest disappearing. Among these I fondly remembered my professor's departure and his death latter and the marriage of my colleague Sushma Nanda. All these were put together and a fond student from Pilani, Shekhawat, drew pencil sketches to every piece based on my theme expressed. On some of these, in fact, a detailed prose form was attempted and abandoned.

Here I intend to give a few examples of the genre I was developing at that time.

ECOLOGY

The Neo God

Each organism gives what it can
And takes what it needs
Patience is extreme,
When lost anger irreversible
Cause here effect there
Cause now effect later,
Everything is connected,
It is powerful, it is fragile,
Some one prepares food,
Some one consumes,
Someone else nourishes
It is useful, it is harmful
Thus commons are strengthened
for common good.

EXPECTANT

Two palms over the abdomen
Moaning to mitigate the pain
A life of limbo inheriting
The child in the belly protesting
The cot carries the wife of Amir
In the ominous kerosene flicker

The nameless begetter weary
His job shorn of the other day
Slams the door and spits the floor
Sits in a forsaken corner
Musing over the unwelcome bastard
Addition to the shoal of slaves!

The thoughts struck the fair
A distant groan at the frontier
A line of lightning passed the airs
The stars closed the shivering eyes
And count the passage of moments
A shriek of thunder winters the torments

Million pairs of hands varicose
Come forward and demand bellicose
Piercing the darkness of night
A twin arms of delivering might
A child in health born in filth
To break the fetters of age-old strength

The sight of the scene frightened
The humid heart of the dispossessed
Turns back in diffident dismay
To peep through the damned doorway
Nursing the hopes forlorn
The nature of the new born

WHO ARE YOU?

Who are you?
Oh who are you?

You came to me with the sails of breeze
When my breath was ebbing in the air
You brought me the masts of direction
When my life was tossing in the Spasm of despair

Who are you?
Oh who are you?

The wandering crescent
Behind the veil of clouds
The resplendent starlet
On the descending firmament
The raising gait of the wave
In the coying mists of ripples
The flamboyance of the dancing bubble
In the infinity of the ocean
Compass of the stranded traveler
Candle in the fortress of darkness
Cataract of the dew
And the serenade of the palm

Who are you?
Oh who are you?

The symphony of the calls woke me up
The message landed in my yard
They flew from me in the morn
And nestled in yours at the dusk

Oh heart of my heart
And mind of my mind
You are my bloom, and
You are my spring

TO THE OTHER BANK

The lamp that shone in my life
The flicker that kindled hope against hope
Waned and vanished in despair
The grotesque fears in the candle - less life

Clarion that moved into action
Raised its voice as a maestro
And lost its stretch into oblivion
The ill tuned voices from the stranded string

The pervasions of the Bunyan shade
Impelled me from the serpent vile
The stray wind stormed the trunk
At the ken are the colourful shades of life and death

Across the river I am
Coursing on a dauntless boat
Haunted by darkness, death and distress
Struggling their way onto me

My journey over the ferry, arduous and exacting
The dance macabre of shadows and cymbals
Foundered and found vent into darkness
At the glitter and glare of the splashing revolt

Misted out at the streaming sight
Of the raising beacon, littled into
A mystic vapour while I anchor my voyage
On the sum of light, love and life

Surprised at the new dawn
Eagerness and relief inquired where
Did I go last night. Thundered on the sky............

SANTAL WOMAN

A santal woman looks at herself.
Half naked, bare footed and bones mocking
The shriveled hair bundled into a bun of patience
And over her hips a basket wealth of compassion

The santal woman gazes behind.
A police dances at the ashes of her hut
A marauder plays music for the dying victim
And a jackal watches wistful with its moist tongue

The Santal woman searches herself.
The ragged garments flew to wipe the tears
The naked feet walked fast to help the lame
The bared bones marched to relieve the hunger

The santal woman raises from the slumber.
Repels adaptation and rejects the detachment.
A woman aroused is stranger than the devil.
And a weak aroused is mightier than the evil.

The santal woman rediscovers herself
The deep forest drew her toward
The basket carries the breath of men
The grenades within left a smile, a trail of venture

PRICE AND THE VALUE

I know
The price I have to pay
For everything I do
For everyone I come in contact
But . . .

I have yet to realise
The value
of anything I am expected to do
Of anybody who comes around me

When I fell
And eagles clamour for my rotten flesh
And dogs quarrel over my hollow bones
When told of this
She said:

What can I do when he is like that.
I am lovelorn
Being so
Must I be forlorn

WHO COMMANDS THE MORNING

Behind the highest walls
In the hardest sandy graveyard
From the witness of opacity
Of the ignoble metal unleashed
Are the elemental powers of fission
Through the wombs of men's brains.

From the pedestals of heavenly cabin
The goods of doom delivered safe
And triggered the ticks of last breath
With invitation descended the death
He who delivered is Homo sapiens
Recoiled are the remnants of ancestry.

Nobel, Lenin and Magsasay
Reduced to annual reminiscences
Prizes, Awards and Pughwashes
Are the sad remembrances
Of the blackest idea
Emanated from the whitest house.

Goaded on by fears, the fears of surrender
Drawn on by hopes, the hopes of conquest
Forced by challenge, the challenge of supremacy
Was created the Elixir, the elixir of elixirs!
But alas! Hanging everlasting
Damocles' legacy of New Mexico.

Gird up your loins
Oh men and women
Heartbeats of the Universe
Hopes of the posterity
Here is the answer
And you shall hearken to it.

Born in the primeval oceans, life and society
Endured the ebbs and tides in part and body
Changing and progressing since the remote millennia
Rose into harmonious unity through diversity
Man the Great, crowns the pinnacle
Is he for the society or the society for him?

Evils are the altruists in travesty
Individualism breeds them besides anarchy
Brothers and sisters, let us not
Bother the dead heaps of static arm-chairs
Who think and revel within the narrow limits
When the world is ever expanding.

With feet anchored in common man's earth
Hands raised into the inviting horizons
Mouths agape with rousing calls
The mountain does not wait for Mohammed
Shall we not hasten the proud waves of society
Shore the new beaches before the dusk sets in?

Gird up you loins
Oh men and women
Admixtures of contradictions
Instrumentals of less rationale
For I ask thee a question
And you shall answer me

Who are the sinners? Scientists?
The mere tools they turned out to be
Their souls throbbing no death and doom
Brain children orphaned and begetters discarded
But how can we ignore Baldwin, when
All the means of deluge are products of science.

Whose default ? For the urge of extinction
Of the atom or the Universe?
Of the death or the life?
Of the citizen or the state?
Of the individual or the society?
The fault lies with the existence of matter!

If not so, then is it of
The Marxian economics or the Freudian sex?
The proletarian discipline or the affluent anarchy?
The cool practices or the holy precepts?
The purpose or the lack of it?
The fault lies in the futility of existence!

TRIUMPH OF HUMANISM

A Homage to Count Stauffenberg
The land of the German is the land of man
The urge of the man is the peace in unity
But the paths of heaven pass through dungeons of hell
And the story of Deutschland is the story of the worl

The decade of sway and storm
Lulled the masses and lured the mound
The mansions of humanity, the toil of civilisations
Bulldozed by the insolence of the madding crowd

Bismarck's agony rose in his grave
To wipe the tears of his forlorn goals
The land of the Germans turns a mother of gallows
Where were no walls, yield no place without walls

The unity of man, the premise of universe
Toned in full throat by the clarion of Goethe
The orient and the occident, the old and the new
Fell to the blinding storms of the meridian blaze

No cheers to Max Mueller, no waves to Keyserling
They are spared for the heroes of Auschwitz
And to the bush above the drunken lips
The melodies of Bach, the beats of heart
Are dried in the din of warlord's drums
Reverence for life is the chosen epitaph for Schweitzer

The science is the anchor of prosperity
The Nazi science is the scaffold for the posterity
The pride of Germany, Oh! Einstein
Your sighs in the barn went unheeded

The atom of the scientist, string of the maestro
The word of the scholar and the whiteness of the horse
When put to abuse by the hordes of Hitler
The glory of the gene rises against the prophets of doom
To remind the world the existence of the other kind

There was a man with the laurels for victory
But itching for the blood of the master, the murderer
The looks reaching far the frontiers of Europe
The nose probing into the depth of depths

The lips as tight as the vessels airtight
And as bright as the hours of sunkiss
The left out eye and the spared fingers ask Stauffenberg:
When the twilight comes, will the sunlight be far away?

When the ropes of hangman
Could not hang the might of Resistance
I but chorus in glee
For the triumph of humanism

GOD: A GREAT NECESSITY

Omnipresent! Omniscient! Omnipotent!

How nice it is to have a God.
No one sees god. But every one feels.
At least it is said

It is like the bird that
'Feels the dawn when it is still dark'.
It is also like the wolf
That feels the dusk when there is still light.

The Pancha Bhootas, of nature were resources
When balanced, but very harmful if imbalanced.
Both good and bad are the attributes of the same.
Humans realised ecology and called it god.

When a child is borne
The mother feels the god.
When some one dies,
The dear ones fear the god.

When someone kills the other without touching him,
the witness sees the god.
God is not merely linkages, but a web, inscrutable.

When bad people succeed and enjoy life,
Why bad things happen to good people?
What is god doing?
Is he existing, or if not is he also bad like the powerful.
God's duty is to protect the good and punish the evil.

An enigma indeed.
God lies in the work.
Work produces dirt.
Cleanliness is next to Godliness.
Truth is god. But truth is bitter.
It takes us to the elegy land,

The last lap of all journeys, sooner.
God is a self contradiction
Myriad times I felt how nice if we have a god Albeit,
Formless, faceless, flavorless,
tasteless, speechless, senseless,
But valuable and powerful?
God is an insatiable yearning.

No one sees god, although feel, but late.
Therefore evils and bads, flourish.
How nice it is to have a God.

I have seen god,
In the first paragraph of
A Tale of Two Cities by Dickens.
And in the entire Siddhardha of Herman Hesse,
In Do Bigha Zameen taking Balraj townwards
And in Boot Polish when
David sings for rain, in Jail!

I feel god, whenever good happens,
Rain and river banks
I deny god, whenever bad happens, heat, dust, villainy
This is the stuff of god, a summation of all probabilities

But GOD has always haunted me
and did not enlighten me.
Ecology enlightens me.
And I found my God.
A great necessity.

If there is no God Invent One
Voltaire

CHAPTER - 9

CONFINES OF HOBBYING

HOME WORKS
HOSPITAL WRITINGS
SRI SRI'S MAHAPRASTHANAM
PRANAB RAY
CUT AND PASTE
MY POETRY
ART OF SHEKHAWAT
AN INHUMAN VISITOR

A. HOME WORKS

Triumph of Humanism

During the 1965-66 session I joined German classes. Learning a foreign language was a requirement for obtaining a Doctorate! Our Professor Lothar Wendel was a man of culture. His house was a Library-cum-Photo-museum I was often his guest. He embarked on writing a small book on German Civilisation. He wanted a tailpiece –a poem on his heroes – Herman Keyserling and Count Stauffenberg and offered his library for reference. After perusing for some time I picked up a few books, notably, Soldier's Revolt by Wolff. It tells the failed attempts on the life of Hitler by a group of highly decorated soldiers led by Count Stauffenberg who was then in the intimate trust of Hitler. It failed when some one inadvertently pushed the briefcase with the bomb from his vicinity to a distance. Bomb exploded. But Hitler escaped with minor injuries. Conspirators were shot by a firing squad in a Quadrangle at the Military Headquarters in Munchen.

The piece was written as a Homage to Count Stauffenberg who wanted to save the German Nation from its own leader!

Expectant

I used to walk every evening with Pranab Ray, my close friend and a classmate in Chromatography, Micro-biology and Pharmacognacy classes and a few friends to a small local market - 'Connought' Place. During these times we would discuss current affairs of India and world.

He was a student of M.Pharm, a distant nephew of Satyajit Ray but an admiring associate of Utpal Dutt in Calcutta. One day he was narrating the stories of Muslim infiltration from East Pakistan, flourishing Madrasas and the rise of religious fanaticism. We felt it was going to be a future menace, which became prophetic.

What is the remedy? Revolution – communistic - the one that brings all communities together. But what was going on in Bengal was merely rhetoric, theory, idealism without ability to transform. That was why the Naxalbari revolt that followed from this time, failed. Harekrishna Konar and Harikishen Singh Surjit, who returned from a secret trip from China, after meeting Mao also did not realise the basic ingredient of ushering a revolution – other than secrecy and doctrines. – The Physical Strength! And roping in the otherwise unwilling Muslims into the movement was felt a necessity. Lack of Leftism by and large among Muslims everywhere became a historic scourge on the world, though communism in India was heralded chiefly by Muslims led by Muzaffar Ahmed, among others! So Karim, a Bangladeshi, and his yet to be born son became our topic-a futuristic piece appreciated by Ashim Chatterjee whom I met in Pranab's home a few years later. Incidentally the name Karim belongs to a dear classmate in my college.

Santal Woman

Those were the days of rumblings in the left-front in Bengal soon after their historic win in the elections. Marxist cadre were asking for sweeping reforms.

Bhadralok were prevaricating. Suspicious of them began in the minds of people, yearning for better deals, especially in the North and Eastern regions. The latter were well populated by the original people, the so-called tribals. The fiercely independent Santals. Jangal Santal became a rallying point. They were using women and children for confidential communications to avoid police repressions. Many such stories and sequels were narrated to me by my friend Pranab Ray, and asked me to write on them. The result was this piece.

Pulse of Life

In 1965, Padmanabha Rao joined Commerce Department as a Research Scholar, resigning his lecturer post in Jedcherla, to do his doctorate under Dr. Dool Sing, who returned from MIT, USA after a two semester exposure.

He once told me of a great colleague to check our curiosity levels. Sure of this, he placed a Magazine, "Srujana", in front of us. Many glanced, perused and left. I persisted in going through. He told me of its Editor - his colleague at Jedcharla College. I subscribed for it and also for a few friends. In a later issue, he read a piece, Jeevanadi, authored by his friend, loudly. I was not impressed. He goaded - Why not you recite – a challenge clothed as a request – diplomatic as he was always. I did. He acknowledged I did better. The author, editor and his colleague was Varavara Rao.

One day, alone, I was reciting it loudly, pacing the room. Some friends – Pillai, Pranab Ray, Surendra Singh and Trivedi liked the rhythm, here and there. But how to explain the meaning, as they want. Another came in.

I explained line by line. They wanted a translation. I translated line by line; wherever English equivalents were wanting friends helped. The meaning of each stanza came out vividly, and in totality it was satisfactory. It read, progress is inevitable, it goes on, no matter the hurdles and breakdowns, the beats of hearts never end.

All dispersed. Soon after some sadness descended on me from far away Brahmin society. Helpless, returned to the room in Ram Bhavan. Wept for a while as was my frequent relief in those times. Took their scribbles, wetted a while, substituted some words. Everything fell in tune. Pranab came and saw - the only one so far. Varavara Rao today is a Communist Revolutionary. A great soul. During Emergency I had to burn all the old issues of Srujana, a great little monthly. Sadly.

B. HOSPITAL WRITINGS:

Spontaneous and Emotional

I was carried at midnight by my friends to the hospital suddenly afflicted by Gastroenteritis. When the body is weak, dehydrated thoughts go astray. Helplessness brings fond memories of lost people and sends us despondent and activates tear glands. At this juncture what passes on through your mind and heart tells you what you are! After an initial stay of a week, after several months, I had to be again hospitalised for another week. In all these 15 days, I must have read a few books and wrote considerably almost every day. They constitute about 10 pieces, retrieved in this collection.

Who Commands the Morning?

Dr. Choksi, sympathetic to my plight gave me a book, a great narration by Pearl. S. Buck, the American journalist and novelist, Nobel Laureate. It dealt with the Atomic Bomb Project carried out in New Mexico Desert under the leadership of Oppenheimer. The world's top scientists who took part in that were the characters in that. It was here that Oppenheimer exclaimed at the detonation and compared it to the Sun described in the Vedas! This was my inspiration for - Who Commands the Morning? My forebodings then, as an young man of 23 years with stars in the eyes and - of Nehru, came true ultimately – much to our chagrin and sorrow.

Others

One day, some one in the ward passed away, his young wife weeping inconsolably. Her hell began. A day letter the one on my side too died. Routinely the body was taken away, no one wept but for cutting sorry figures. There was enormous sadness descending on me. Dr. Choksi gave me another book, the God that Failed – It contained the tales of people like Koestler and Andre Gide who were led to communism by idealism and were frustrated by its practices and denounced it in later years. It was an eye opener to me – one who was gradually gravitating towards it in the very heart of the Citadel, a great capitalistic – Pilani, the native place of Birlas.

No matter what one does on this earth, one day it looses its value and even memory. No matter what you dream, realities could be different. But one has to keep on doing as per one's conscience. For this everyone needs a vocation, a hobby, an ideal dear to the heart, irrespective of livelihood chores. If both are same or match, life could be wonderful, for, one is seized by a passion all the time. Such feelings made me write a long prose that fell into poetic cadences, gradually.

By then I failed to enter the army as an Officer, in two attempts with SSB; then the goal shifted to become a Professor like my Godfather, B N Muley. This too appeared slipping with his death.

They shifted me to the children's ward. My neighbour was one Saboo, a student from the school, a scion of an industrialist family. Most of the time he will gossip about his friends and asks me what I was reading and writing. This rare curiosity, I never found again, that too coming from a boy born in riches and live and die in riches, only. Yet so much interest in people around. Doctors and Nurses thanked me for retaining him on his bed. Otherwise, he would be on rounds. Jayant Gupta told me that this boy requested the authorities not to inform his parents, lest they would carry him to Delhi, but wanted to be treated in this hospital.

C. SRI SRI'S MAHAPRASTHANAM

Inspirations and Translations many, only some remain

As I mentioned earlier the arrival of Padmanabha Rao as a research scholar brought considerable changes in me. One day he showed me a book, a slim one, Maha Prasthanam, The Longest Journey, written by Srirangam Srinivasa Rao, popularly known as Sri Sri, and asked me to read any page. Until then I had not heard of this collection of poems of different genres. He asked me to read loudly, then I found that they had a rhythm with in. I did not understand the meanings of many words. I read more pages, then loudly. I enjoyed it immensely. Thus, I got hooked to that book, and forever. Sri Sri became my Guru. And Padmanabha Rao who introduced me, became a Guruji, ever since to me and several others.

It became an encore, a routine for me to read the poetic pieces loudly every day in my room when no one was around in the hostel corridor in Ram Bhavan. One day Surendra Singh came to see me and heard it from outside. Pleasantly mischievous, he brought some friends to listen to me from the vicinity. Thus, began another chapter in my daily chores. Some friends would come only to enjoy the style and rhythm of my recitation and imitate me, to poke fun. But some asked me to tell the meaning, and others to translate. Gopala Krishna Pillai and Sweta Kurup told that the pieces resembled Vallathol, the great poet in Malayalam; Basant Tiwari felt they resemble compositions of Ram Dhari Singh Dinkar; Shahabuddin said Sahir Ludhianvi wrote similarly. Pranab said similar writings came in Bengali from Srikanto Bhattacharya. His poetry was also recited loudly, set to music and then to dance, subsequently. My friend Kanchan Mojumdar told me that they came as cassettes and CDs. I had the good fortune of seeing a young man performing a fantastic dance to a revolutionary song of SriKanto. Alas! Srikanto died at 25! Coming back to the main stream of narration. This pastime lead me to translate some of Sri Sri's Poetic pieces. Among many recited and translated, whenever demanded by friends, I could retrieve from my archives only some! They are here:

D. PRANAB RAY, A Junior, but a Mentor

In a few cases it has so happened that Pranab told me a story, a theme, and I wrote as heart-felt as possible; improved it and then split into poetic notes. Then the vocabulary and figures of speech. Santal woman, Expectant etc, come in this category. The large varieties too – essays modified into poetic design. Pranab was a great asset and creative to core.

E. CUT AND PASTE

One can write tellingly. Another can write movingly on some subjects, as pet themes and certain times. Then scissor the prose into pieces, of smaller dimensions. Yes, a poem is made!

MY POETRY, ART OF SHEKHAWAT AND AN INHUMAN VISITOR

Most of my poetry was written in Pilani. In those years I was also asked to teach. One student who is an artist like his father before was so much fascinated that he volunteered to make sketches appropriate to each poem. We together laboured to make poems hand written and he would make sketches with pencil. A marvelous book emerged by the efforts of Shekhawat.

The book traveled with me everywhere and admired by everyone who saw it. But in Pondicherry it disappeared. Some heartless student or a visiting teacher just pilfered it with a smile. Most sins are committed with the force of smiles and the gullibility of the victim!

CHAPTER - 10

A COMMA

Recapitulations
My plans for all
Talents, Ideals Monsters
Dreams, Hopes, Wards, Relatives
Railwayline, the last straw
Tail Pieces
Journey Continues

Two paths diverged in the woods,
I took the one that is less traversed by,
And that made all the difference.

ROBERT FROST

RECAPITULATIONS

I became qualified to do Masters with the financial help of many good people. I won credentials to appear before Services Selection Board to become an officer in the army directly by my own efforts. I earned two qualifications for the first time in the history of the college, which is meant to train only to get a single one. I also developed Reading habits - books, periodicals and newspapers, literature and society. From these habits, sprout two faculties – to view things from more than one angle; to analyze objectively, using all tools in questioning, the 6 Ws.

But the family, how big no one knows including Engels, thought typically. Extra learning is extra burden, wasting extra time, in livelihood matters of house-holding where I am a resource. The family influences my thoughts in my plans for their development. This is alien to them, interests alone count. All families are blinkered.

Family responsibilities are two types. What they desire and expect me to work for. What I wish of them and work for. In both they do not work! In between come interferences from others. If these three coincide, it is a heaven in attendance. Suppose they do not, it is a hell that pursues until the end of life. Without emotions and

Freud, without economics and Marx, and without motives and commerce, no life exists and runs.

With education ignorance goes and innocence gives way to new thoughts on gradually increasing subjects, where objectivity guides. One steps out of pasts, through outlooks and insights.

MY PLANS FOR MYSELF AND MY FAMILY

I always felt that all my brothers and sisters should be post-graduates, taking me as a role model without spoon – feeding, with Amalapuram as the base, because it is a familiar ground. I wished to make a permanent residence in a familiar region in Konaseema. All these take time and determine the livelihoods, marriages and families which are my responsibilities. To fulfill I must obtain the highest qualifications to finance our progress. According to them, I should settle in a livelihood, add to it through a marriage, keep all together releasing one by one – permanently working for and worrying about finances, guided by the Matriarch and her comrades from the system when education was not there. Time is not to be respected, only the interests.

TALENTS AND IDEALS APPEAR MONSTERS

Inheritance from two grand fathers is telling. One was a Sanskrit traditionalist, grew reformist in time valuing traditional culture, literature and advocating their exposure to the forbidden sectors in society. Another was an English-educated Nationalist, innocent enough to be exploited by friends and relatives. Therefore I am given to sensitivity despite all disadvantages of remoteness to communications, poverty and false pride of a Brahmin society, I survived and moved only with the help of innumerable good men and women. I was lucky to be born in the later Gandhian times and to have studied during Nehruvian times when Humanism was still not extinct.

All contradictions and paradoxes constitute a suffering. I learnt here and Pilani that my sufferings are not limited to me but spread in society, which made me one in the milieu. This outlook gradually turned me into a socialist and ultimately a Marxist. Most others think conversely and become self-centered, while I identified with the sufferings of others. This made all the difference in later life.

Thus I was exposed to many authors and books such as Premchand, Abbas, Sadat Manto, Somerset Maugham, Herman Hesse, Andre Maurios, Ayn Rynd, James Baldwin, Bertholt Brecht, and ultimately confused! In Telugu, Ranganayakamma, Sri Sri, Gopichand were my favorites. Naturally I became useless in worldly matters. These were facilitated by the library which was representative of India and books were carefully selected at Pilani. We read others to learn their experiences, their views and future thoughts to check whether or not we are on right lines.

DREAMS AND HOPES, WARDS AND RELATIVES

By the time one thinks that formal education is completed and must go for earning a livelihood and become a house holder, One must have passed through a series of changing desires. In the school I wanted to be a history teacher, because I liked the teacher of history. In the college it is a different story. Initially I wanted to become a journalist and work against injustice. This also was found to be a passing fancy. But the streak does remain. Further I needed a good job quickly to support my family. Thus I concentrated on NCC. I not only passed my degree in second class but also obtained a 'C' certificate in NCC qualifying to enter the army as an officer directly. That my efforts failed at the last post, is another story and sad at that.

When we completed the degree, there were only Five who qualified for further studies. Two went for M.Sc in Zoology, one went for M.Sc in Botany, and two for Bachelors in Education. My relatives wanted me to become a typist or stenographer after matriculation. Now they also wanted me to become a teacher and begin earning before the age 20 and marry within the family another earner so as to support the rest of the family.

My mind and heart were very gregarious – always wandering in new pastures. Thus I came to Pilani. New avenues opened up. A research field in India or in the west, or entry into Central Services stared. Both are very competitive not always compatible with merit. I opted for research towards a Ph.D and further although friends opined differently. Many people felt that I would have cleared the UPSC, but this did not enter my system even after visiting the Administrative Staff College at Mussorie. I regretted this my whole life!

Therefore I have put everything into the research field to obtain a Doctorate despite many apparently un-surmountable hurdles. I was dreaming a great career in science with several role models known to me and desirous of becoming one. When I was ready to jump into the wide world with a Ph.D and with some additional faculties of heart and mind, the outlook was quite rosy with unknown expectations. I wanted to be like more than my professor, obtain the fellowships of all the three academies in India; desired to be at least a shade of Haldane, Salim Ali and Kosambi. I wanted to change my society. Alas I could not influence even my family, none wanted higher education similar to mine I could not improve them enough for the changing society. I was allowed only to maintain patience and fortitude and wait to witness my own stagnation.

I was rejected by one and all. Mother and siblings kicked me after benefiting on the quiet, for not serving like S G K Murty, calling it ideal; First wife unwilling to contribute to my efforts after benefiting enormously and indulging in treachery as a parting gift; Colleagues suffering from envies and the like; Students deserting for gaining worldly wisdoms after obtaining benefits, Authorities fearing my correctness and honesty. I was more idealistic, therefore, impractical. I do not regret. I am proud of these. All these, which happened, in the years to come could be fore told!

Final Product was a fateful Synthesis of all experiences, focus-less, but a versatile personality, rare in these times: Grand Fathers' Simplicity, Justice, Fair-plays; Goodness and Work, Poetic Prose, Questioning, Analysis, Sensitivity, Broad mind and large heart, honesty are all mine! Tear Shedder,A Piner and A Longer, yet a worker! But a failure, nevertheless. A lower middle-class member.

I wanted to know more and more. I wanted to learn by listening and reading. I wanted to change, change the society. I could not even change my mother, from whom I learnt most. I could not convince her that ignorance and innocence go with education give way to new thoughts and actions. Such people become role models for others to follow. But she went back to Gopalam model where one works and distributes the growth to others, retaining them as slaves, They need not work, just be obedient to the master atleast apparently. The only role model for a family of several scores, thus remained excluded from all of them for ever. What is the use of education and knowledge? The custodians of Vidya and Gnanam, the Brahmns, themselves were antagonistic of me! For opposing internal marriages, permanent labors of the eldest sons, and supporting the philosophy of Role Models and role of books in all these evolutionary issues.

Hindsight wisdoms prevent blinkered views with full stops,
And promote fullest views with commas.
What a destiny that my ecosystem too is falling,
in the name of development.

RAILWAYLINE, the last straw

This project is ill-conceived. Harmful to the local people; Could be profitable for some vested interests. Ecologically not studied about its consequences. There will be exoduses of people into Cotton Seema,

Commercialization of everything here. People will leisurely repent. When all rivers were bridged so that all the beauties of this delta can be relished, why the railway. What needs to be done in this area was to improve the water bodies – rivers, canals, tanks, storm drains, Intertidal zones - improve the waste lands into fertility and restoration as was done in some parts of Antarvedi and not increase investments with money bags! Madness overtook all common senses. When cotton completed the dam and the delta was organized there were terrible migrations into. After the railway, migrations with adverse impacts begin.

TAIL PIECES

My grand father went to every house known to him in Visakhapatnam, showing the photo of his grandson receiving the Doctorate Degree from Shri G.D. Birla and Dr. Dharma Vira, the then Governor of West Bengal. He foolishly convinced himself that his failed life may re-green through his grandson, recovering some prestige and self respect.

Alas, my siblings not only refused to emulate me but blamed me for not supporting them, falsely, like their role model did to his siblings. For this, why this role model had to go to a University and do a Masters ? When I went further and farther shall I continue going heights or march into their cellars considered heavens by most.

They did not realize strengthening myself helps them strengthen. To increase this impact they too strengthen themselves in the lines of their eldest brother. This must be told by a mother. She did not. End results were counter productive blaming me as the arch villain of their lives and spreading this canard wherever possible! With a vermillion mark on forehead and sandal paste somewhere, one can do any crime or sin! Mark of Cain is that powerful.

JOURNEY CONTINUES

I believe that everyone must write his/her story. If the first part is childhood and education, the second is employment and interactions in society. On retirement one ruminates, memories keep coming. Sometimes one feels bad about oneself. And sometimes very gratified. One feels contented. And sometimes sad. These opposites fill our lives, Mostly we do get opportunities to undo only a few. With such an insight into life, which we get just once, every one must write one's journey and one's memories, and every one else must read them !

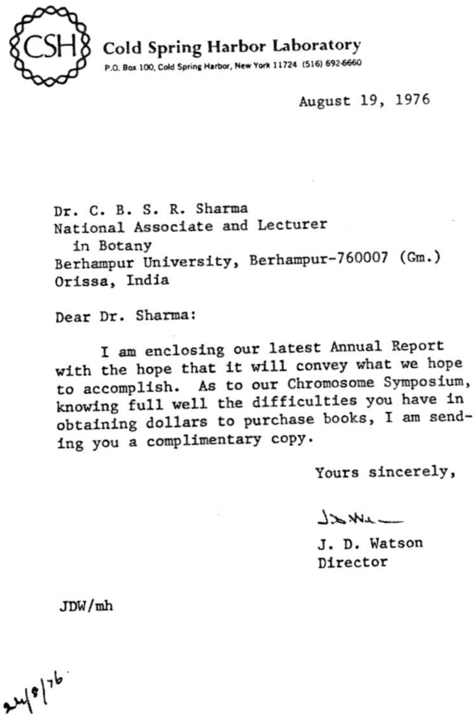

Cold Spring Harbor Laboratory
P.O. Box 100, Cold Spring Harbor, New York 11724 (516) 692-6660

August 19, 1976

Dr. C. B. S. R. Sharma
National Associate and Lecturer
in Botany
Berhampur University, Berhampur-760007 (Gm.)
Orissa, India

Dear Dr. Sharma:

I am enclosing our latest Annual Report with the hope that it will convey what we hope to accomplish. As to our Chromosome Symposium, knowing full well the difficulties you have in obtaining dollars to purchase books, I am sending you a complimentary copy.

Yours sincerely,

J. D. Watson
Director

JDW/mh

24/8/76

Fig. 25. Latter from a Nobel Lauseate.

Fig. 26. Head, the Heaviest.

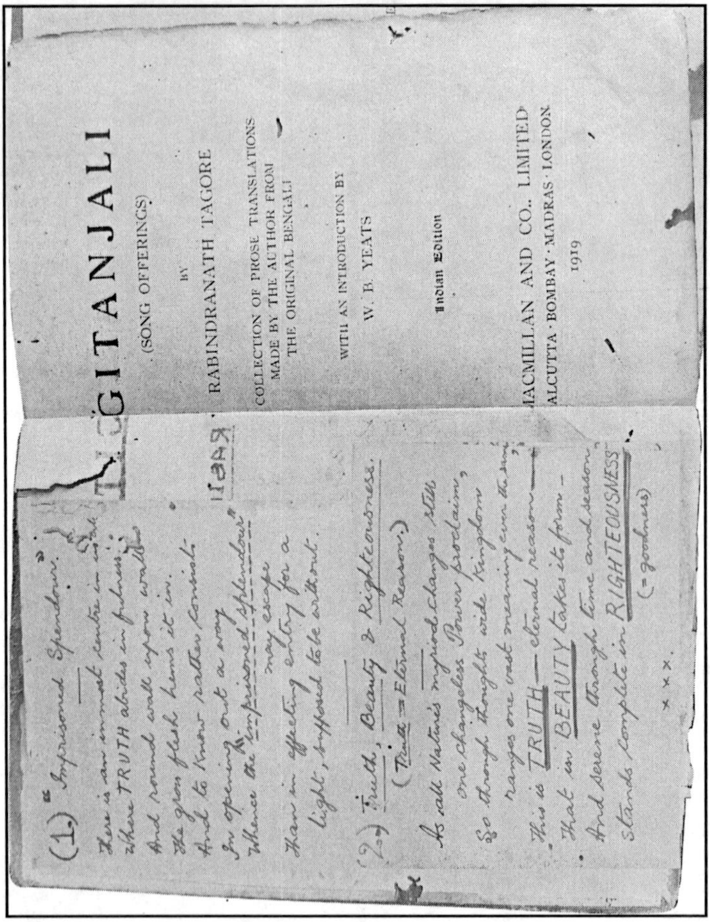

(1) "Imprisoned Splendour."
Here is an inmost centre in us all
Where TRUTH abides in fulness;
And round wall upon wall
The gross flesh hems it in.
And to know rather consists
In opening out a way
Whence the imprisoned splendour
may escape
Than in effecting entry for a
light, supposed to be without.

(2) Truth, Beauty & Righteousness.
(Truth = Eternal Reason.)
As all Nature's myriad changes still
one changeless Power proclaim,
So through thought's wide kingdom
ranges one vast meaning ever the same.
This is TRUTH — eternal reason —
That in BEAUTY takes its form —
And serene through time and season
stands complete in RIGHTEOUSNESS
(= goodness)
× × ×.

1931

GITANJALI
(SONG OFFERINGS)
BY
RABINDRANATH TAGORE
COLLECTION OF PROSE TRANSLATIONS
MADE BY THE AUTHOR FROM
THE ORIGINAL BENGALI
WITH AN INTRODUCTION BY
W. B. YEATS
Indian Edition
MACMILLAN AND CO., LIMITED
CALCUTTA · BOMBAY · MADRAS · LONDON
1919

Fig. 27. Notes on Gitanjali by the Author's, grand father

LINEAGE OF PATRIARCHY
Gene Flows and Genetic Drifts

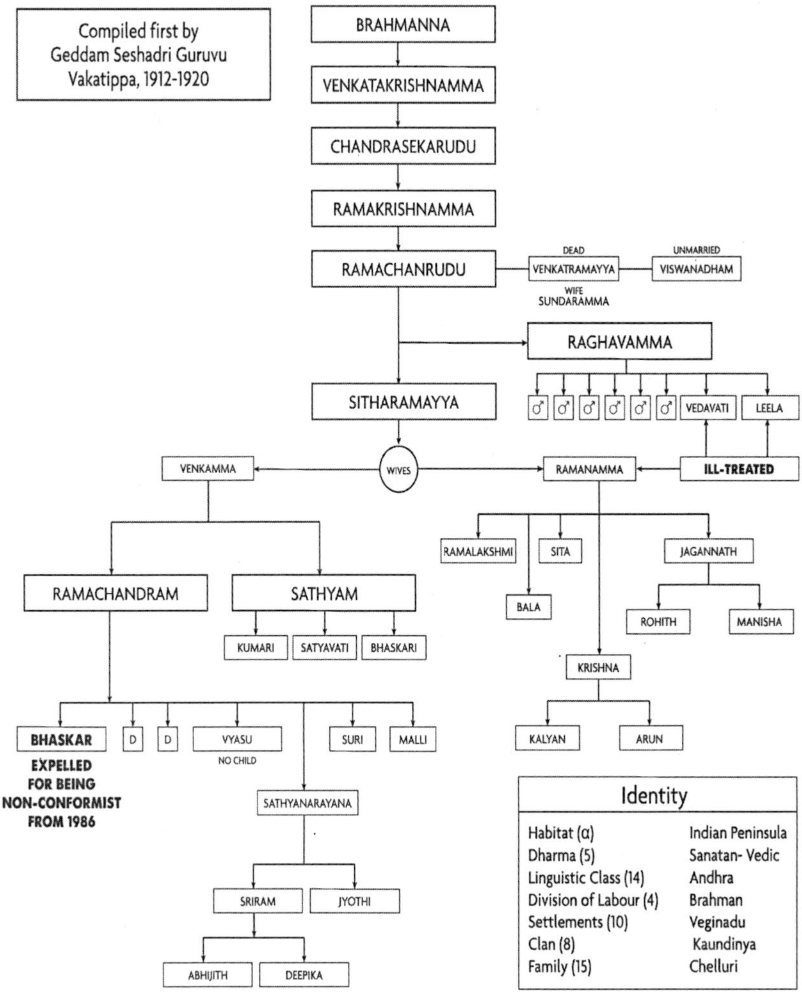

Fig. 28. Family Tree of the Author
Vamsam as a concept excludes the Female. Therefore wrong.
Characters continue for 7 generations.
Consanguiny disturbs all principles and calculations.

Fig. 29. Sitharamaya – Author's Grandfather.

Fig. 30. Author, 50 Years Ago

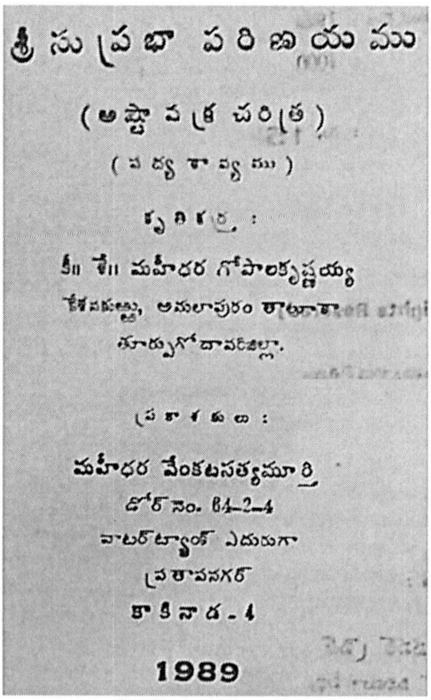

శ్రీ సుప్రభా పరిణయము

(అష్టావక్ర చరిత్ర)

(పద్య కావ్యము)

కృతికర్త :

కీ॥ శే॥ మహీధర గోపాలకృష్ణయ్య

కేశనకుర్రు, అమలాపురం తాలూకా

తూర్పుగోదావరిజిల్లా.

ప్రకాశకుడు :

మహీధర వేంకటసత్యమూర్తి

డోర్ నెం. 64-2-4

వాటర్ ట్యాంక్ ఎదురుగా

ప్రతాపనగర్

కాకినాడ - 4

1989

Fig. 31. Ashtavakra Charitra was authored by my Maternal Grandfather about a century ago and published by his last child in 1986

APPENDICES

Detailed Contents
Author's other Books
Companion Volumes
Author's Biodata

1. DETAILED CONTENTS

CHAPTER 1 : MY ECOSYSTEM

First books read
Stranded in an island surrounded by water
Allergies

CHAPTER 4 : COLLEGE DAYS

Pre-university course, an experimental batch
3-year degree course, an experimental batch
Teachers and students
Library
Sesha prasna
Field trips: long
Field trips: short
Field trips: voluntary
Seemingly un-surmountable hassles?
Ajanta's money orders
Suranna pedananna
Vedavati and leela
Addiction-1: the n c c
Subedar ajaib singh's advice
Progress card – non-recognition
The rss\
Blitz and karanjia
Nehru, socialism, krishna menon and localism
Panchsheel and revolutionaries
Abbas & other regulars
Penchant for rhetoric and polemics
Investigative journalism
Counter weights
R k narayan
Values vanish, the shop closes
Most important pastime: cinema
Avidi and my fathers death
Some personal experiences
Non-recognition of merit repeatedly
Frugal living
Hunger strike
Attractive girls
Some unique women
Unprefered as a future son-in-law
my likely helpers

CHAPTER 5 : UNIVERSITY LIFE IN PILANI

Eashwari khushalani and ambuja pillai
Some incidents during research tenure
Fancies and tit-bits
Muralidharan the palmist.
Porous rcc
Padmini's uniqueness
The epic journey for nothing
Job hunting – TIFR, BARC, universities, Subbarao-chemistry, I I SC.

CHAPTER 6 : ERRANDS ALONG THE GANGA

Delhi
Tenneti and nalini mohan
Chanchal kapoor and mendel centenary
Services selection board
Jaipur – hawa mahal, amber palace
Muzaffarnagar
Bajpayee, chandrasekar, tarakeswari sinha
Two notable visits
shahid ahmad siddiqui and deoband
Delhi, agra, lucknow, aligarh
Calcutta, on several visitations with pranab ray
Belur – dakshineshwar,
Sibpur
Alipore central jail
College street, rabindra bharathi and red lights
Nabadweep : krishna consciousness, jayadeva &geeta govindam
Ashim chatterjee and his admirers and followers
University at ballygunge

CHAPTER 7 : BACK TO ROOTS

a munikhanda of brahmins
row of seven banyan trees- a heritage site
the village tank – another heritage site
literary and culture personalities
pandita jagannatha rayalu of moghul court
saraswatula ramayanam by ramasastry
my grand father's library for children
cadaver service by my grand father

CHAPTER 8 : HOBBYING ON EMOTIONS AND ABILITIES

CHAPTER 9 : CONFINES OF HOBBYING

ART OF SHEKHAWAT
AND A HEARTLESS VISITOR

CHAPTER 10 : A COMMA

What am I – a recapitulation
My plans for myself and my family
My burden : reading, waste of time
Dreams and hopes- relatives and realities
Railwayline, the last straw
Tail Pieces

2. AUTHOR'S OTHER BOOKS

1. **SHARKS ON CAMPUS, Tragicomedy of Indian Universities, p. 371, 2015. - Notion Press**
   A compilation of all articles published from 1967 onwards
2. **ECOLOGY, ENVIRONMENT AND POLITICS, p. 412, 2018. – Gyan Books**
   A compilation of all my lectures mostly in other Universities
3. **TEACHING LABOURS OF SISIPHUS. VOL. 1. p. 425, 2019. - Gyan Books**
   Class Room Lectures of 5 Subjects I taught in 4 Universities
4. **TEACHING LABOURS OF SISIPHUS. VOL. 2. p. 381, 2020. - Gyan Books**
   Class Room Lectures of 5 Subjects I taught in 4 Universities
5. **IRRIGATION TANKS OF SEMI- ARID ECOSYSTEMS. p. 393, 2020. - Gyan Books**
   Field Report on irrigation Tanks, under a DOEF-MIDS project.
6. **GLOBALIZATION and ECOPHAGY – 1,**
   Chemicals, Mutations and Gene-Epidemics, Gen-Next, p.204 2020
   Impacts of Mutations on society
7. **SO THE TIME PASSED AWAY. p. 92, 2021. Gen-Next**
   Heart Beats bared after 55 years
8. *AUTOECOGRAPHY OF STOLEN FUTURES-1* **- Gyan Books**
   Modern Piranhas and Uncertain Tomorrows

If Health Permits, the following Files may also become Books

9. GLOBALIZATION and ECOPHAGY – 2
   Styrene Episode at Vishakhapatnam. A Repeat of Bhopal Gas Tragedy ?
10. *AUTOECOGRAPHY OF STOLEN FUTURES-2*
    Working with bulls and dozers in Institutions
11. *AUTOECOGRAPHY OF STOLEN FUTURES-3*
    Analysis of crimes and Criminals in Universities
12. ECOGRAPHY OF COROMANDAL COAST
    Conservation for Development and Development for Conservation
13. PIRANHAS ON PROWL IN THE EDUCATION SYSTEM

3. COMPANION VOLUMES

COMPANION OF THE PRESENT BOOK - 1

PIRANHAS AROUND
Bulls, Dozers &Charlatans

COMPANION OF THE PRESENT BOOK - 2

PIRANHAS EVRYWHERE

Higher Education more hazardous
than the black waters of
Orinoco in Amazon

COMPANION OF THE PRESENT BOOK - 3

PSYCHOANALYSIS OF PIRANHAS

Chicanery And Neosorcery

4. BIODATA OF THE AUTHOR

Studied : BITS, Pilani, IISc, Bangalore, Worked : ICAR, Universities of Berhampur, Madurai, Coimbatore and Pondicherry, Visited : USA, UK, Hungary, Thailand, Malaysia Resource : DOEF, MHRD, UPSC, UGC,

---

I. PROJECTS

1. Monozite Belt Floristics -UGC
2. Maize Germplasm Collection for CYMMYT at Mexico – FAO
3. Medicinal Plants used by Tribals of Phulbani District, Orissa - UGC
4. Drugs with Heavy Metals : Genetic Toxicity in Rodents - ICMR
5. Pesticide and Fungicide Mutagenicity in Plant Systems – CSIR, UGC
6. *In situ* mutagenicity; *VCs and Colleagues destroyed this, mid stream* - DOEF
7. Small Water Bodies : Most Satisfactory and Appreciated Work - UNDP
8. Ecography of East Coast of Tamil Nadu : INTACH, CAG, & PU
9. Vision 2020 Pondicherry, MSE, GOP

@ Assisted by Many Students– 15 obtaining M. Phils., 6 Ph. Ds + 2 [**N Balasundaram, G.Ram Prasad** [*de facto* **Guide**], and 8_'Political' Exits : **Radha Saraswati, Vishnupriya, Sridhar, Manivannan, Shivanna, Mary Rani,** Tejoprakash, Ilangovan [Most treacherous]]

II. PUBLICATIONS RESEARCH

India : 50+ Developed Countries; 30+ [USA, UK, SWITZERLAND, **ITALY, HOLLAND, GERMANY, HUNGARY, JAPAN, AUSTRIA, CZECHSLOVAKIA] in Cytogenetics, Mutagenesis**

PUBLICATIONS ARTICLES: 50+

in Hindu, Indian Express, Down to Earth, University Today, Caravan

PUBLICATIONS REVIEWS : 6, on Chemical and Pesticide Mutagenesis UK =2 , USA =2, Malaysia =1, India [CSIR] =1 = INTEGRATING INTO A BOOK [5]

III. WORKS AS BOOKS

Published:

1. Sharks on Campus, p. 371, 2015, Notion Press : Popular Articles
2. Ecology, Environment and Politics, p. 412, 2018, Kalpaz : Popular Lectures

*3. Teaching Labors of Sisyphus, p. 807, 2019, Gyan in 2 Vols : . Class Lectures

*4. Irrigation Tanks, p. 393, 2020, Gyan [with Others] ; Field Work-1

Finalizing : Research Works, 2020

5. Environmental Mutagenesis and India -1. Keeping Aspidistra flying with concepts on Genetic Changes
6. Environmental Mutagenesis and India -2. Genotoxic Ecosystems and a Polymer Accident at Visakhapatnam
7. Environmental Mutagenesis and India -3. Genepidemics and Covid-19, preceded by some and Awaiting many.

Under Processing

*8. Ecography of Coromandel Coast for Development and Conservation Leads -Field Work-2

9. PLANTS as Medicines, Energy, Pesticides and Monitors
10. Piranhas on Prowl and Pervasion : Comi-Tragedies in Indian Universities : Observations
11. Stolen Futures : Auto-Ecography of a decimated Teacher [2 Vols], Experiences
12. Ecology & Environment, as if students matter: A Treatise in 6 Volumes : Library Exercises
    1. Applied Ecology 244p
    2. Ecosystems 201p
    3. Biodiversity 305p
    4. Natural Resources 350p
    5. Pollutions & Toxicology
    6. Destructions and Recoveries 183p

IV. WORKS AS COLLECTIONS

1. Books, Journals, Magazines : to be donated [PU Library = 800, Faculty = 80, Others ?]
2. CD ROM containing News Paper Clippings on Environment for about 15 years : Inability to do

*Extensively Pirated by Colleagues

Selected Publications In
Cytogenetics, Mutagenesis and Allied areas

In Developed Countries [out of 36]

1. Chromosome Information Service7 27-28.1966, Japan
2. Chromosome Information Service 21 : 8-10. 1976,
3. Cytologia 33 : 94-96. 1968, Japan
4. Cytologia 34 : 112-117 1969
5. Experientia 32:1465. 1976, Switzerland
6. Biol. Plant. 19 : 150-152. 1977. Czechoslovakia
7. Mikroskopie (Wien) 33 : 30-34. 1977, Austria
9. Z. Pflanzenphysiol. 84 : 163-166. 1977, Germany
10. Beitr. Biol. Pflanzen 53 : 211-215. 1977. Getrmany
11. Caryologia 31 : 89-93. 1978 , Italy
12. Acta Biol. 29 : 189-191. 1978, Hungary
13. Mutation Res. 46 : 19-26. 1977, Holland
14. Mutation Res. 67 : 161-166. 1979
15. Mutation Res. 76: 341-345. 1980
16. Theor. Appl. Gen. 55 : 253-5, 1979 , USA
17. Mutation Res. 91 : 333-336. 1981
18. Toxicol. Lett. 18 :195-203.1982, Holland
19. Environ. Exp. Bot. 23 : 79-83. 1983, USA
20. Biol. Zbl. 102 : 567-70. 1983, Germany
21. Biol. Zbl. 102: 571-576. 1983
22. Cytologia 48 : 749 -52, 1983
23. Cytologia 52 : 365-371. 1987
24. Cytologia 53 : 255-261. 1988
25. Biol. Zbl. 109 : 303-306. 1990
26. Biol. Zbl. 109 : 307-311. 1990
27. Mutagenesis 5 : 105-25. 1990, UK
28. Critical Reviews in Plant Sciences. 9 : 409-442. 1990, USA
29. Agroecosystem Instability due to pesticides (in) Integrated pest management (ed. Tait & Napompeth), West View Press USA: 92-96. 1987
30. Pesticide induced gene-epidemics in the Third World countries. (in) Global Development and Environment Crisis - Has Humankind a future ? (ed. Idris) : 642-662. 1988
31. in situ detection of genotoxicity - Possibility and Measurements (in) Mutation and the Environment [eds.Mendelsohn, Mortimer L & Albertini, Richard J] Wiley-Liss Inc. Part E : 67-76. 1990, USA

In India [out of 51]

1. Indian J. Biochem. Biophys. 8 : 324-326. 1971
2. J. Sci. & Ind. Res. 30 : 571-587. 1971
3.
4. Curr. Sci. 46 : 55-56. 1977
5. Ind. J. exp. Biol. 15: 940-941. 1977
6. The Nucleus 24 : 60-65. 1981
7. Curr. Sci. 50. 278-279. 1981
8. Indian J. Exp. Biol. 20: 97-8. 1982
9. Curr. Sci. 52 : 1000-2. 1983
10. Envi. Mut. Soc. Newslet. 8:1-14,1985
11. Proc. Ind. Acad. Sci. 96 : 303-309, 1986
12. Biology Education. (UGC): 39-41, 1986
13. Acta Bot. Indica 21:238-243. 1993
14. Bionature 13 :169-177,1993

In Conferences, Symposia, Seminars

15. The exotoxin from Bacillus thuringiensis. A new spindle and cytokinesis inhibitor with probable mutagenic and anti-neoplastic potentialities. In : Symposium on Mutagenicity, Carcinogenicity and Teratogenicity of Chemicals, Department of Atomic Energy, India (1975): 63-73. 1976
16. Plant monitors of Environmental Mutagens In: Workshop on Evaluation of Mutagenic and Carcinogenic potential of Environmental Agents. Environmental Mutagen Society of India, BARC, Bombay. 27-39. 1982
17. Urban mutagens - Ecological approaches to monitor low doses and complex mixtures of environmental chemicals. In: Indo-FRG Seminar on Methodological approaches for estimation of low dose effects of radiation and chemicals in the environment. Department of Atomic Energy, Bombay (1983) : 204-212, 1984
18. Environmental quality assessment. Role of higher plants in the understanding of genotoxicity of pollutants. In: Recent Trends in Botanical Research. (ed : R.N. Gohil) Scientific Publishers, Jodhpur: 237-48, 1984
19. Mutation pollution : Plant indicators in situ (in) Plant Science Research in India: Present status and future challenges (ed: Trivedi, Gill, Saini) Today and Tomorrow Publishers, New Delhi, 15-23. 1989

20. Environmental Factors in the spontaneous aneugenesis in Plants (in) Environment and Genome (ed. S.B. Bhattacharjee), Saha Inst. Nucl. Phys. Calcutta. 64-75. 1991
21. Genotoxic pesticides may cause imbalances in the agroecosystems (in) Environment and Biodegradation (eds: Agarwal and Rana) Society of Biosciences. 69-79. 1992
22. Developmental and reproductive toxicity, Clastogenicity, Aneugenicity and Mutagenicity of pesticides in barley progenies and onion meristems (in) Genetic Toxicology in India [Ed: P.S. Chauhan], Envi. Mut. Soc India, 101-10, 1996
23. Genetic Consequences to human society from energy technologies. Do chemicals pose greater threat than radiations? [in] Energy Crisis and Environment [ed : Xavier et al] Loyola Institute of Frontier Energy, Chennai, 343-349, 1997
24. Genotoxic ill-health from the pollution of ecosystems, human occupations, habitations and consumption – Monitoring and Management in India [in] Ecology, Environment and Natural Resource Management [ed: Tahir & Hussain, Jamia Milia Islamia], 7-24, Jawahar Publications New Delhi, 2003

Abstracts [out of 44]

1. Cytological effects of some Vinca Alkaloids. Proc. All India Congress of Cytologists and Geneticists, Punjab University, Chandigarh: 80. 1971
2. Cytogenetic hazards from fensulfothion, Dexon (DAPA) and its degradation product dimethylphenylene diamine (DMPDA) Mutation Res. 53: 247-248A. 1978
3. In situ Cytogenetic monitoring of vegetation around Hindustan Polymers factory, Vishakapatinam, India. Environ. Mutagen., 5, 409. (abs) or 415, 1983.
4. Genotoxicity of the Municipal sewage of Madurai, A South Indian City. Environ. Mutagen 182: 77. 1986
5. in situ genotoxicity monitoring of sewage habitats by animal denigens and experimental plant systems. Ann. Meet. Env. Soc. (USA) 19: 1988
6. Use of Native Plants and Insects as indicators of in situ Genotoxicity. Proc. 5th ICEM, Cleveland: 182, 1989
7. Water Hyacinth (Eichornia crassipes) is an excellant in situ monitor of aquatic genotoxins. Proc. 5th I.C.E.M. Cleveland; 182. 1989

8. Possible breakout of genepidemics in Asia. A hypothesis on the predominant role of pesticides (in) Nat. Symp. Nuclear Techniques in the Study of Pesticides in Food, Agriculture and Environment, University of Agricultural Sciences, Bangalore 8-10 Feb, p. 2, 1989
9. Ecosystem Genotoxins - Indicators and Concepts. M.S.S.Research Foundation, Madras, May 1992
10. Ecosystem Approach to the management of traditional irrigation systems. [in] Congress on Traditional Sciences and Technologies of India. Section : Water management. Indian Institute of Technology, Bombay. 28 Nov-3 Dec, 1993
11. Reconnaissance on the East Coast of Tamil Nadu - Survey on the status of wetlands and potable water for evolving conservation and development strategies [in] Symposium on Conservation Restoration and Management of Aquatic Systems, I I Sc., December 9-13, p108, 2002.

Articles in Print Media = 50+,

Lectures in 35 Universities = 120

INDEX

C

D

E

H

I

L

N

Q

R

S

T

U